Just Get Over It!

We All Have A Choice

By Susan Lugli

Just Get Over It!

By Susan Lugli

Copyright © 2010 Susan Lugli

This book was published in the United States of America.

Library of Congress Catalog Card Number: TBA

International Standard Book Number: 978-1-453-75484-9

Cover Photo By: Ken Daly

"Susan writes with power and sensitivity. You will smile at her clear insights into Life. And as time passes, you will realize how deeply her words have continued to lift you in encouragement and to challenge you to a happier life. Do yourself a favor and read this often."

-Kent Whitaker
New York Times bestselling author of *Murder by Family*

"I could never have lived through that!" is something many of us have said when hearing of a friend's trauma, but Susan is one who has lived through unbelievable experiences. They include physical harm that end in a miracle of healing and have propelled her into a ministry of hope. You will be inspired by her words of encouragement and feel that your problems are not so bad after all."

Florence Littauer
International Speaker and Author

"Susan Lugli is a wonderful writer, sharing stories of her triumphs over tragedies. Her courage in surviving mental illness, abandonment, and a fiery crash inspires readers to make choices everyday to live life with hope, joy and enthusiasm."

LeAnn Thieman
Coauthor *Chicken Soup for the Caregiver's Soul, Chicken Soup for the Christian Woman's Soul* and 8 more *Chicken Soup* titles

"To my wonderful family, and the friends who stood beside me through the good and the challenging times of my life."
~Sue~

Introduction 1

Out of the Fire 3

GROWING UP 11

The Sadness of a Little Girl 12

The Shoes 18

The Wonders of Vicks Vapor Rub 22

Identity 25

I Can't Help Falling In Love 29

The Love of My Life 33

The Reunion 35

The Destruction of Suicide 38

My Father 42

The Look of Deception 47

GROWING THROUGH ADVERSITY 50

What Was Your Name? 51

Empty Nest 56

The Heartbreak of Drug Abuse 60

Choices To Make Me Grow 65

Desires of Your Heart 69

A Gift for a Season 72

My Spiritual Mom 76

Building the Walls 81

GROWING THROUGH PAIN 84

Give Thanks 85

Hero Unaware 88

Hope From the Ashes 91

God Supplies Angels 99

Sisters In All Seasons 102

God's Answer to Prayer 106

I

REAP WHAT WE SOW 109

MY EXPERIENCE AS A BURN SURVIVOR 113

VICTORS NOT VICTIMS 118

HURT BUT NOT DESTROYED 120

GROWING BEYOND THE CIRCUMSTANCES 123

MOVING OUT OF HIDING INTO FREEDOM 124

THE THREE TRANSFORMATIONS OF RUSTY 127

WHERE TO LOOK, WHAT TO SAY 135

THROUGH THE EYES OF CHILDREN 138

THE JESUS IN ME 142

THE BEST TIME IN MY LIFE 144

MY FRIEND DICK 147

OLD FRIENDS 153

DEPRESSION 155

NOT A COINCIDENCE 157

THE PAINTING 159

THE ACHING HEART OF MARY 162

LITTLE CHURCH ON THE RANCH 167

SPOOKY 169

HORMONE MADNESS 172

WE MADE COOKIES 175

MY HEARTBEAT 176

BREATH OF LIFE 178

BE STILL .... **ERROR! BOOKMARK NOT DEFINED.**

DIVINE ERRORS 185

PUBLICATIONS WITH SUSAN'S INSPIRATIONAL STORIES 188

CONTACT SUSAN LUGLI 189

Introduction

My passion is to share the short stories I have written about the different stages in my life. Hopefully, you can identify with the journey, recognize where you are, and be inspired.

Many of my short stories have been published in other books, magazines, and newspapers. My goal is to put them all in one book to share with my family and friends. Short stories are meant to stand alone, so they require knowing basic facts that may be retold in several of my stories included in this book. Over time, God has given me a different understanding as I grow in my walk with Him.

My purpose in writing has always been to share the good, bad, and ugly in my life so that you can be encouraged in whatever place you are. I want to express my feelings as I have grown into the woman I am today. I pray many of you will recognize those same feelings and know you are not alone.

My journey may be similar to your own. I want you to know we all must make a choice how we will react to the circumstances of our lives. I have chosen the title, *"Just Get Over It,"* because in my life, I had to do just that in order to go on living. I kept looking forward to what God had ahead for me. In Jeremiah 29:11, NIV, God promises, *"For I know the plans I have for you,"* declares the Lord, *"plans to prosper you and not to harm you, plans to give you hope and a future."*

I pray through reading these stories you will understand that you too can go forward and not get stuck in your circumstances. Don't let anything keep you from growing into the beautiful person God wants you to be!

- Susan Lugli

Out of the Fire

I awakened from a sound sleep as I was thrown across our motor home. Dishes crashed all around me. "Did we hit gravel?" I wondered. In an instant, a wall of flames separated me from my husband, Rusty, who was driving, and our twenty-seven-year-old daughter, Nikki, in the passenger seat.

Intense heat chased me away from them. I pleaded with God to save us all or none of us. I spotted a gash in the side of the aluminum wall of the motor home, and I kicked my way through it. Even though I wasn't on fire, I could see my skin melting from the intense heat. Blood ran down my forehead and into my eyes, blurring my vision as I tried to escape.

The grass in the gully where I landed was on fire. As I crawled away from the motor home, flames pursued me. I crawled to a wire fence and tried to climb it, but fell back because my feet were burnt and raw. I was only wearing shorts and a t-shirt. Two men suddenly appeared across the fence and picked me up like a sack of potatoes, racing from the menacing flames. "Save my family! Save my family!" I screamed. Billowing black smoke blinded me as our motor home was incinerated. I collapsed, sobbing, sure that Rusty and Nikki had been burned alive since the seats where they had been sitting just moments before were rapidly consumed in the inferno.

The events that swirled around me filled me with feelings of panic, desperation, and abandonment, much like I did as a young girl of eight when my mother died as she was holding me in her arms. I couldn't save her, and now I couldn't save my family either.

Rusty, Nikki, and I had been heading north on I-5 near Corning, California, on our way to Washington that Saturday, August 28, 1993. Rusty had pulled off the road onto what looked like the shoulder, but was really a gully hidden by tall grass. Our motor home careened into the gully, landing at a tilt. We didn't know until later that the gas tank had been punctured.

As I lay there, a policeman leaned over me and said, "Your family is up on the road. They are alive." Then I heard a paramedic say, "Let's take the man first," so I knew Rusty was in the most danger. We were taken by ambulance to Chico Hospital to be stabilized. From there, Rusty was taken by helicopter to UC Davis Medical Center in Sacramento, while Nikki and I stayed in the Chico Hospital emergency room.

My hands and body were swelling to twice their normal size. The emergency room nurse had to cut off my wedding ring to keep it from being embedded in my burned flesh. She had no way to know the depth of my sorrow as she cut away that symbol of our devotion. As she snipped the band of gold and carefully removed it from my left hand, all I could do was cry.

For our first twenty-five years of marriage Rusty had spent his time chasing his dreams of business success. I'd spent my life trying to be the best wife and mother I could be. I'd raised our two kids, Nikki and Todd, and run our twenty-five acre ranch on my own. I'd tried to create the kind of family that would make us all happy. I had known there were other women, but dared not make an issue of it. Knowing he was unfaithful only drove me to redouble my efforts to become more of what I thought he needed me to be. But my marriage was lonely, so I let the Lord fill my emotional needs. He was the husband I longed for when Rusty wasn't.

Shortly after celebrating our twenty-fifth wedding anniversary in March of 1990, Rusty decided to leave me and file for divorce. After much prayer, tears, and counseling, I gave Rusty up to the Lord and tried my best to learn to be a godly single person. By July, I was sure our marriage was over. I felt sad but relieved, confident God still had a good life ahead for me. It was a difficult time, but it was also exciting – a time of growth and hope for the future. By August, however, Rusty was having second thoughts and talked about coming back. I wasn't completely sure I wanted that anymore.

Rusty went through a time of depression that brought him to his knees. He finally surrendered his life to Jesus. Then he started sharing his heart with me for the first time. By October, I reluctantly agreed to work on our relationship. At first I worked on our marriage only out of obedience to the Lord, but as I saw Rusty's commitment, my heart softened towards him. By February, I was truly excited about our new life together in Christ. That new life made me hope we could have a new marriage, too. On our twenty-sixth wedding anniversary, we had a full wedding ceremony to renew our vows before family and friends. Rusty put the wedding ring on my finger, looked into my eyes, and said, "Wear this ring as a token of my love."

Our marriage became the marriage I'd always longed for. We were friends and lovers, sharing all of life, enjoying the fruits of our labors together. Then the accident happened. Two years and five months after he placed that ring on my finger, the emergency room nurse cut it off. Was this how our marriage would end?

I didn't have time to ponder the possibilities. Once I'd been stabilized, the helicopter that took Rusty returned to take me to the burn unit. Nikki wasn't burned but severely injured with a broken back, broken arm, and dislocated knee. The doctors decided to keep her at Chico. As they were taking me away, I could hear Nikki screaming and crying for me. Everything inside me wanted to go to her, to hold her, and comfort her. But the burns covering my body and threatening my life made that impossible.

News of our accident spread fast. When I arrived at UC Davis, a few close friends and relatives were already there. They told me other family and friends were holding a prayer vigil on our behalf. I'd been a devoted Christian for more than twenty-five years. God had always seen me through, and I trusted He wouldn't let me down now.

When I was settled in the burn unit and finally lucid enough, they told me I had a broken back, with burns over 48% of my body. My prognosis was poor – but Rusty's was worse. The doctors gave him only a 9% chance of survival. Rusty was semi-comatose, fighting for his life three rooms from my own.

There were days I wanted to die because the pain seemed unbearable. I endured numerous skin grafts and excruciating bandage changes. The pain never went away despite the strong drugs.

As I watched from my hospital bed, the seasons changed from summer to fall. Friends and relatives continued to visit, but they were going on with their lives while we were stuck in a life of uncertainty and relentless pain. I tried to be thankful that my family was alive, but I became more depressed with each passing day.

Cards and posters covered my walls reminding me of all the people who were praying for us. Friends and family took turns rubbing my forehead because that was the only place I could be touched without it hurting. They urged me to eat, kept me company, and were simply there for me. The tape recorder was my constant companion; I listened to worship and praise songs, along with the Bible on tape. Listening to these helped me focus on something other than the painful procedures necessary for my healing. The nurses waited for me to pray before every bandage change; they even learned the songs I sang.

Rusty needed a miracle to survive. I continued to love him and pray for his recovery, but I simply couldn't bear to see him. I struggled with such conflicting emotions. I didn't want him to die – I couldn't imagine life without him – but if he was going to die, I wanted to remember him as the love of my youth. I didn't want to mar those precious memories with images of him burned, swollen, and hooked up to machines.

Rusty's doctors kept insisting I see him soon in case he died. I kept refusing. I was determined to wait until I knew he was going to live. As I learned more about the severity of his injuries, I accepted the possibility of his death. Our doctors said we would know – one way or the other – by mid-October.

Almost every morning, I recorded a message for him so he could hear my voice and know I was okay, even though he was still unconscious. I chatted about who came to visit, sang him little songs, and told him how much I loved him. The nurses would take the tape recorder to his room, play the tape, and return it to me – often with tears in their eyes.

My rehabilitation was long and painful. I had to wear a brace that encased my body whenever I was in an upright position. Apart from the burns, my broken back required surgery to fuse it together. I later learned that 85% of people with similar injuries end up as paraplegics.

My Bible verse for rehab was, *"I can do all things through Christ who strengthens me"* Phil. 4:13, NKJV. I said it over and over. This was especially appropriate because "all things" was precisely what I had to learn to do over again. I had to relearn how to feed myself, walk, wash my face, brush my teeth, and even go to the bathroom. When I was released from the hospital on October 3, 1993, six weeks after the accident, my niece, Vicki, moved in to take care of me around the clock for the next five months. I chose to leave the hospital without seeing Rusty still fearful he might die. But Rusty didn't lack visitors. All our family members and a few select friends visited him faithfully and continued in prayer.

October 15 proved to be the turning point the doctors predicted. Rusty almost died that day. When he pulled through, the doctors assured me he would live. After that, I agreed to see him. Our twenty-five-year-old son, Todd, came from his home in Dallas to be near us. He and his wife, Gena, stayed at our house. Todd took pictures of Rusty so I would know what to expect.

Our friend, Don, wheeled me into Rusty's room in the burn unit, with its familiar smell and sounds. I went to his side and watched him as he slept. He was still unable to move or respond. He was burned over 68% of his body, part of his left ear was burnt off, left eye destroyed, face badly fractured, and four fingers of his left hand

8

amputated. They didn't know if Rusty had brain damage from his severe head injuries. He was still semi-comatose.

I felt peace surrounding him, but longed to be able to hold him. He was so broken, swollen, burnt. I longed for him to be able to live the active life he had. Don anointed him with oil, and we prayed together. We didn't stay long. I was glad I finally found the courage to go, but struggled with the realization that Rusty was so badly injured.

Rusty regained consciousness and recovered enough to come home on December 22, 1993, just in time for Christmas. A young man who was like a son to us, Frank, became Rusty's primary caregiver for five months after he came home. I was glad to have him home, but missed our life before the accident. After our marriage was restored, we'd become close in every way - including physical intimacy. I couldn't help wondering if we'd ever have that kind of closeness again.

During the first year after the accident, we slept in separate bedrooms because of our pain and our need to get good sleep. It was so lonely with him in one bedroom and me in another. There was another kind of loneliness, too, brought on by our different healing rates. My rehab took about all the patience I had. I didn't think I had the patience to help Rusty through the recovery process as well. I was ready to move on to my next stage of recovery. I found it difficult to wait for Rusty to learn to live all over again. He woke up without realizing what I'd gone through. It was difficult, but we both adjusted.

I took over Rusty's care from Frank five months after he came home. By the grace of God, I found the patience to help Rusty make the transition from being a burn victim to becoming a burn survivor.

Sometimes I felt like Rusty's mother, encouraging and motivating him when it took so much of my strength just to encourage myself. It was a sad and weary time in my life, but the moments came when I could see improvement. Rusty's progress and my own made the hard work of recovery worth the effort. Our struggles, emotionally, physically, and spiritually, drove us to prayer. And God faithfully answered our prayers, day by day, as He healed us. Little by little we beat the odds – and are continuing to do so.

Five years after the accident I could do almost everything physically I did before, even riding my bicycle. My physical challenges came from my back injury that caused limited movement and pain. Rusty had several operations in his program of plastic surgery. Nikki occasionally struggled, both physically and emotionally, but we were all moving ahead. We were still miracles in progress.

Rusty and I have learned many valuable lessons through these trials: Our love for each other has deepened. The devastation on the outside of our bodies has allowed our inner beauty and strength to come out. And we don't take anything for granted anymore.

God has brought us out of the fire – scarred but strong – to be a testimony of His faithfulness, with our love purified, our faith refined, and our priorities in order. I give Him the glory.

My first article was published in "Today's Christian Woman" with Connie Neal September/October 1998.

Condensed in "Holding On To Heaven while Your Husband Goes Through Hell" by Connie Neal 1998.

Chapter One

Growing Up

> As I think back at the beginning of
> my life, I try to remember the good
> times. I chose to be happy instead
> of sad no matter what the
> circumstances

The Sadness of a Little Girl

I was all tucked away under the warm covers lying tightly against my mother. She had been sick for most of my eight years. We were visiting my Aunt Shirley in Chicago and waiting for my father and older sister to arrive from our home in California. Just that afternoon the sun had been warm in the back yard, and we had laid on the grass together watching the clouds and feeling a gentle breeze on our faces. Mother would spend hours telling me stories, brushing my hair, and laughing at my silly knock-knock jokes. I knew when she did not feel well, but on this special day she had been outside with me playing and laughing. I always tried to make her happy and did everything I was told so she did not get mad. As we lay together, we talked about going to the beach at Bodega Bay. How she loved watching my sister and me climb the rocks for hours. Then every Fourth of July, we would go to Clear Lake camping. We threw sparklers to see their reflections in the lake after it grew dark.

She loved sewing our clothes and curling our hair to look pretty for Sunday school. We went to the Methodist Church in Santa Rosa, California each Sunday as a family. For my first eight years, I felt secure in our home. Living in a happy family with my older sister, father, and my mother was a wonderful beginning for a little girl. Now as my mother held me in her arms lying in the bed, she quietly died of heart failure. I remember screaming for my Aunt to come and help. I begged my mother not to leave me. Her last words were, "Be a good little girl." God had given me a gift that day of a happy last time with my mother.

My father arrived a few days later and our lives had changed forever. My sister screamed with anger. My father stood in shock. My aunt begged him to leave me with her, but Dad insisted we stay together. So we took my mother's body to be buried in Chillicothe, Ohio where most of her family was located. Then, we journeyed on to Columbus, Ohio where Dad had grown up. He had ten brothers and sisters that could help him raise my older sister and me. Poor Daddy tried so hard to care for us and to keep his butcher job. I tried to be good while my sister became very rebellious. I had wonderful teachers who would send goodies home for us. They would make me costumes for school programs and Halloween outfits. I don't ever remember a time when I did not feel love around me.

Dad would punish me when I deserved it but would always say, "This is going to hurt me worse than it will hurt you," and I believed it did. He always cried right along with me. He told me every night when he put me to bed how much he loved me.

Finally, I was sent to my Aunt Coral's to be safe. My sister was quite violent, and Dad needed my aunt to watch over me while he worked. She was still angry about losing Mom and took it out on me. I loved being at my aunt's during the week and cried when I had to go home. When I was there, I felt part of a family and secure.

I went to many different schools and made friends quickly, but my reading skills fell behind. I was held back in third grade to try to catch up.

My life at my aunt's house was happy until I turned twelve. Once again, someone I loved died. My uncle had a heart attack during the night. My dear aunt went into shock and could no longer take care of me, so I moved back to my father's house.

Not long after I returned, Dad married a woman with one daughter. My new stepmother let me know right away that she only had one daughter. She was quite cold and unloving. Her daughter, Jackie, was the same age as my sister, and we grew very close. I think she liked having a little sister. My older sister became very jealous of our relationship.

Soon, my father was making plans to move us all back to California. He got a butcher job in Millbrae where we lived in an apartment over his work. I remember the first Christmas. Jackie and I put on our bathing suits, went up to the roof of the apartment, and lay in the sun. We both wrote letters to our friends in Ohio telling them about our suntans. I went to Taylor Junior High in Millbrae and made some good friends. My best friend's name was Loretta. Her Mom and Dad liked me so they had me over a lot.

I always loved children so I ventured out one day to get some babysitting jobs. I made up flyers with my name and phone number on it and put them in doors in my neighborhood. Before I knew it, I had a lot of jobs and was able to buy some of my own clothes instead of having everything hand-made by my stepmother. I think I was the only girl in the locker room with a homemade bra. Just when I was getting settled in our new surrounding, Dad got a new job in Sonoma, California.

I started high school there. Once again, I needed to make new friends. I found some babysitting jobs with some of my teachers. My favorite was Bob Bergman who had an adorable little boy named Robin. Mr. Bergman also had a friend from college named Rusty that dated my sister a few times. He was pretty nice and worked at Palms Inn Resort during the summer. I worked there too, babysitting for their guests who stayed there. By the time I was seventeen in my junior year of high school, Rusty and I had become good friends.

My stepsister, Jackie, was going to be married that June. We were all excited. Dad and my step mom were not getting along very well so Jackie and I were talking about my coming to live with her. She and Bob had fixed up a little house. We were not sure if our parent's marriage would end up in a divorce. I did not want to be in the house alone without her. She protected me when the fights would begin.

I remember the Sunday a week before the wedding. Jackie was going to church with Bob, and I was going to another church in town. We kissed goodbye and laughed about something. She told me they were going on a motorcycle ride to Napa after church. Later that afternoon the phone rang, and I heard my stepmother scream. The next thing I knew, my parents were going to identify Jackie's body. A drunk driver had hit them. Jackie died instantly while Bob was in serious condition at the hospital. I immediately went into shock, as I stood alone in that empty house. I wondered over and over, "How can this happen again? I'm only seventeen and everyone I love dies!"

A few days later as I stood in the funeral parlor being forced to look at the body of my sister, I screamed in disbelief. She was so broken! They tried to make her look like her picture. To me it did not look like her at all. My friend Janet was with me. I kept saying, "This is not my sister. She is not dead. Where is she?" I fainted over and over trying to make this nightmare end.

Rusty arrived from San Jose University, but I was inconsolable. My real sister was married and now lived overseas. Within one month, my stepmother left us to move back to Ohio. My father, who had experienced too much loss in his life, was put into a mental institution. I knew I needed to stay close to my father, so a family in town kept me until my father was able to come home again.

During my senior year of high school, Rusty and I decided to get married. I knew it was not for the right reasons, but I didn't want to be alone. By March I was pregnant and married. I wanted to finish High School. Rusty was working and living in a town thirty minutes away, so we saw each other on the weekends. I chose to live at home with Dad until I was graduated. I hated to leave Dad by himself, as he was not right mentally after Jackie was killed. Not long after I left, he became homeless, jobless, and a lost soul.

As I think back at the beginning of my life, I try to remember the good times. I chose to be happy instead of sad no matter what the circumstances. My mother told me to be a good little girl; and I learned that if I did what she said, I was wanted and loved by most everyone.

That is except for the one I really wanted - my real sister, Sharon. We were never close again after our mother died. My sister was always jealous of me and I believe never got over the loss. She committed suicide at twenty nine when I was twenty six. Someone important died in my life every four to five years between the ages of eight and twenty-six. That included my mother, uncle, stepsister, one miscarriage, two stillborn births, sister to suicide, and my father-in-law.

I had my father's love, and a great beginning with a wonderful mother. I was blessed with parents that taught me to be positive, and more importantly, taught me about the love of God. He was Someone who would never leave nor forsake me.

The Shoes

Over half a century has come and gone in my life, yet I still remember my Aunt Shirley saying, "Look with your eyes not with your hands." In other words - DON'T TOUCH! This was my mother's favorite sister, and we were going thousands of miles from California to Chicago to visit her. Our circumstances for the visit were not joyous, but I tried to be on my best behavior. I was eight years old and my mother was dying from a heart condition.

Mother was excited to see her sister, and my eyes were wide with anticipation of adventure. My aunt had a wonderful large home with the most amazing collection of little porcelain shoes from all over the world. As I stood beside the little wooden shelves filled with shoes, I was once more reminded to look and not touch. I had never in my short life seen anything so beautiful. Each had its own story to tell. Some were made of leather, some wood, others pewter, but the most ornate was porcelain with delicate glass lace. There were men's, ladies' and children's shoes, boots, and clogs. For the first days we were visiting, these one-of-a-kind tiny treasures mesmerized me.

My father and sister were driving to Chicago to meet us, and then we were going on to Ohio together. We were moving to Ohio to be near my parent's families. My mother was very tired so she was in bed most of the time. On the fourth day mother was able to be outside with me. I remember her laughter when I would say silly things and do summersaults on the grass. It was a very happy day - a day that God gave us as a gift. Later that same night she died. I begged her not to leave me. My dear aunt tried to help her to no avail. My mother slipped away from us as we clung to each other.

Life was very sad for me living without my mother but she instilled the love of God into me at an early age. I learned that the Lord will never leave me and I can depend on Him for all things. My faith grew right along with me. Family was very important to me, but by the time I was twenty-six years old, I had lost seven close family members. This included my Aunt Shirley who died five years after my mother. I never forgot those beautiful little shoes on the shelf and the sad bond we shared.

Father moved us back to California and I no longer had contact with my mother's family. I would send Christmas cards, but they were never answered.

I took a trip to Ohio in 1991. It was hard to remember the names of my mother's sisters and brothers, but by researching their names, we soon found them. My enthusiasm was great. I was on a mission. One name was familiar so I called the number. When the lady on the other end answered, I said, "You probably won't remember me." I took a breath and she said, "Is this Susan?" It was like she was waiting for me to call. It had been at least thirty years. I immediately went over to see my Aunt Georgia and was able to video her as she talked about my mother and the past. I was told of my Christian heritage and how my grandfather would teach the Bible. He would sit on his front porch and people would come and learn. No one in the family touched their food until grace was said. She even still had a latched potholder I had made her when I was a child. This gesture made me feel like I had been wanted and loved.

We visited the cemetery together, and there were ten graves side by side. My beloved mother lay beside her favorite sister, Shirley. Even though they had all passed away, I felt excited that I had finally found my family. Two weeks after that special day, Aunt Georgia passed away.

Two years later, I returned to visit my last remaining aunt. She was living in my grandmother's old house on Lillie Street. My long-lost cousin came running out to meet me. We hugged as if time had not passed. As I walked in and saw Aunt Edna, whom I hardly remembered, I felt a connection to my lost past. My eyes drifted around the room. I saw familiar items. There was a picture of my grandparents I recall seeing when I was a child. I also saw a black velvet dress with little pink flowers hanging in the corner. As we talked and laughed my eyes kept going back to the dress. My aunt said, "That dress belonged to your mother." I walked over, took it off the hanger and held it in my arms. I felt the closeness of my mother in that very room. It had been so long, and now I had a piece of her I could feel and smell.

My cousin walked into the room carrying two boxes. "Save for Susan Kay" was written on top of the dusty boxes that had been stored in the attic for over thirty years. He sat them on the floor beside me. I had no idea what could be inside. I opened the box cautiously and carefully. Inside were small packages wrapped in newspaper smelling musty and old. The first one I opened slowly and could not believe my eyes. It was an elaborate little porcelain shoe. My eyes filled with tears as I opened one after the other. My dear Aunt Shirley wanted me to have this wonderful collection of shoes after all these years. As I unwrapped each of the ninety shoes, I thought of the time I looked at them on the little wooden shelves when I was eight. I had wished that I could have such a beautiful collection some day. Now they were mine and a reminder of how much I was loved.

The shoes have given me a piece of my mother through her sister. As I washed each one and rewrapped them carefully, I thought of the stories these little shoes could tell. They all were so different. One of the last shoes I opened was a little brown oxford shoe. As I turned it over I read the inscription saying, "First shoe from Nelle (my mother) 1942". My mother had given this shoe to her sister for her collection, before I was even born.

When I returned to my home, I immediately bought the most beautiful curio cabinet I could find. I carefully placed each individual shoe in its new home so each could proudly show my family's heritage.

After so many years I can see God's divine plan. He was my family. With God's help, my mother and father raised me well. In God's right time, He gave me a wonderful gift of the shoes. They were a reminder of my heritage and the Christian family into which I was born into.

The Wonders of Vicks Vapor Rub

Many years ago I learned of a wonderful cure for almost everything! Picture me as a little girl with bright blue eyes and dark curly hair. I stayed with my Aunt Lucy whenever I was sick. My mother had died when I was eight years old and my father depended on his sister for help. I had a lot of colds and she seemed to be an expert with that illness and knew just what to do. Whenever she would get the cobalt blue jar of Vicks down from the cabinet I knew what came next...YUK!!!

First, she would put it up my nose so I could breathe easier and then underneath my nose too. Next would come my chest where she spread it thick and sticky all over it. Finally, she would give me a big finger full in my mouth for my sore throat. She would even put it on my little cracked toes on my feet. You know the ones underneath and between your toes. Can you imagine what I smelled like? I could have done a Vicks commercial. This product was definitely a wonder rub that my Aunt believed in. And it usually worked, most of the time.

After the cure-all was applied she would sit and talk to me offering me great things like a Coke. My aunt had an old refrigerator on the back porch full of them. In those days I didn't know anyone that had Coke in the house, especially my family. We couldn't afford it. I think back to the combination of Vicks and Coke, it sounds quite sickening.

Aunt Lucy's daughters, Melinda and Phyllis, were a little older than I was. I envied my cousins because I thought they were rich. They had lots of pretty clothes and shoes that ended up as my hand-me-downs. I remember always going home from my sick days with something special. Sunday was the best day to be at their house. On that day Uncle Dwight would take all of us next door to Dairy Queen. It was one of my fondest memories. He would let us get whatever we wanted no matter how much it costs. Guess what I always had...the biggest banana split you ever did see. It was wonderful.

Now that I look back, so many more memories start to appear. Whenever my sister and I would spend the night, all four cousins would sleep all together in the big double bed upstairs. Two were at the top and two were on the bottom with lots and lots of blankets on us. In the era of Elvis Presley, my cousin, Melinda, had posters on the ceiling over her bed. We would lie on the bed, listen to his music, and scream. My favorite things were children, and I was determined to have a dozen, adopting them from all over the world. I had baby pictures all over my wall and named each one. My cousins thought I was crazy.

Phyllis had a best friend named Mary Alice who lived across the field. Now she was really rich. She had her own horse, took dancing lessons, and lived in a pretty house. I was sure she had LOTS OF COKE in her refrigerator! I will never forget the day she gave me her little red toe shoes that she had outgrown. I would dance around my living room and pretend I was the grandest of ballerinas. She will never know what happiness those little red toe shoes brought this little girl who didn't have many worldly possessions.

Many of us as children think back at those times, all having different perceptions of our childhood. To me they were some of the saddest but the happiest times. Those were the circumstances that made me who I am today. Not having a lot as a child made me appreciate everything that came my way. It helped me to learn to budget and persevere through all times. I had to be dependent on God for my every need, so I learned to trust and love Him as if He were my mother.

I will always be grateful for the family God chose for me. There was never a moment I did not feel loved and adored by each member of my family unit. My Daddy would always tell me each night, before I went to sleep, how much he loved me. He would punish me when I needed it and cry right along with me when I was spanked. On my sick days he would get up extra early just to drive me all the way to Aunt Lucy's so I wouldn't be alone. That is real LOVE.

Without those sick days I wouldn't have learned about the wonders of Vicks Vapor Rub!

Identity

Webster defines "identity" as, *"the distinguishing character or personality of an individual."*

It took me many years to realize who the real Susan was. Remember the old series on TV where they would say, "Will the real Susan stand up?" I am now over half a decade old and I am thinking back at my life. I have to wonder what takes us so long to figure it all out?

When I was eight years old the last thing my dying mother said to me was, "Susan be a good little girl." It was not until recently that I realized how those six little words have formed my life. With these important words came acceptance from others who would care for me. As long as I was a happy, good girl everything was going to be all right.

I grew into a woman believing that I needed to make everyone happy. If they were not, it was because I was not good enough. I remember going to a Christian woman's retreat in my late twenties or early thirties. It was like a light bulb went off in my head. I could hear the speaker say, "Are you a God-pleaser or a people-pleaser?" At that time my life seemed to be falling apart. My husband did not seem to be happy and wanted more than I had to give. Our son always seemed out of control with ADHD and drugs. During this time my daughter suffered with depression. What was going on? I tried to be the best I could be. Where was my Hallmark family? As a child I would laugh a lot, be silly, and have fun. Now I was afraid my husband wanted to leave me.

I will never forget the evening I had some friends over for dinner. They had only been with the kids and me, and this was the first time they were meeting Rusty. Through the evening my friend's husband kept asking me if something were wrong. Even late into the night after we went to bed, he called and asked once again. I did not think something was wrong with me, until the following morning when he once again appeared on the porch. He said, I was someone totally different with my husband around. Could I have changed so much in those first ten years of marriage, just to try to make someone else happy? How can one recapture his or her own self after working so hard to please someone else?

Not having a mother as a role model, I decided to use the Proverbs 31 woman as my guide. I studied her and soon started to realize how independent and secure she seemed to be. Those were the two characteristics I needed to work on in myself. My faith started to grow, and I kept hearing the speaker say, "Are you a God-pleaser or a people-pleaser."

I had grown up being a people-pleaser, but now I needed to find a balance in my life. I stopped volunteering for everything to make people like me. If I did not receive joy from doing it, I stopped. From God's Word I learned I must serve with joy. If not, I would be doing it for the wrong reason. So, no more hot-dog lady at the school five years in a row.

My own identity really blossomed after my twenty-fifth anniversary. My husband Rusty announced that he wanted a divorce because he was not happy. I had feared those words for so long. I had been with him since I was fifteen. Now at age forty-four I was on my own for the first time in my life. Our children were grown and on their own. Now I was too. It was difficult, but my faith was strong. I knew God had a plan for my life.

After the first few months I started realizing how positive, happy, and relieved I seemed to be. I had given up all hope that my marriage could ever be saved. I was no longer worried about making someone else happy. I finally woke up to the fact that we are only responsible for making our own happiness. WOW, what a discovery!!!

It was then THE REAL SUSAN COULD STAND UP! She was back after all those years. She even liked who she was and others did too. Remember, that husband? He even liked the new Susan and wanted to work on the very broken marriage. It took months of counseling and a lot of renewing of trust, but GOD DID IT.

It is constant work to keep our own identity. I needed to keep reminding myself in each new stage of my life. When we moved to a family ranch where all ten members of my family lived together in separate houses. I was proud to say our son and his wife pastor a church here in our town. Then I started to become aware of some haunting feelings. I did not know what these uncomfortable feelings were until I went back to visit our friends in our old neighborhood. When I lived there before I was a total individual with my own work and identity. Now, on our ranch we all had the same interests and friends. My children had become my spiritual leaders and pastor. I found I tried to be myself, but recently, I got worried that I would embarrass or dissatisfy them. I wanted my children to be happy, just as I tried to make my husband happy before.

Oh my gosh! I could not let this happen again. It was so easy to slip back into your old way of life. I have worked very hard to be the woman God has formed me to be. He is the only one I want to PLEASE.

Do words like, "Be a good little girl" haunt you? Have they become curses that constantly conjure up that your worth is determined by what you DO instead of WHO YOU ARE?

Does this make you be a people-pleaser rather than a God-pleaser? You are the only one who knows.

I Can't Help Falling In Love

"THEIR MARRIAGE IS A MATCH MADE IN HEAVEN." In some cases this is true, but the road my husband and I traveled tested our love through fire and rain before we discovered that our love was a gift from heaven.

Rusty was twenty-two years old when we met. I was just fifteen. He was working as a lifeguard at the Palms Inn Resort in Sonoma, California. I was babysitting for a family that stayed the summer at the Inn. He thought I was fun, and I looked up to him as the "Older Man." We were such good friends, but my father soon became suspicious of the relationship. Rusty went back to California State University San Jose when summer ended. He was helping his mother run a boarding house to get himself through school. We kept in touch by letters and a common friend from Sonoma.

My home life became very confusing after my junior year of high school. My stepsister was killed in a motorcycle accident and shortly afterward my stepmother and father divorced. Within a month my stepmother moved back to Ohio. All of this was too much for my father to handle, and he was soon committed into the mental institute.

Rusty and I were talking about getting married after I got out of school, but this seemed to be the right time. I had nowhere else to go. By now he was working a construction job in Santa Rosa, California. I traveled back and forth to school each day. 1965 was a very big year for me! I got married, was expecting our first baby girl, Nikki, and graduated from high school all the same year. Three years later our son, Todd, arrived.

Rusty had started a dry wall company in 1964 and became a general contractor five years later. By 1974, he had offices all over the country. We relocated to Sacramento, California in 1984.

I remember my favorite Valentine's Day. I used to say to Rusty, "When I grow up, I want a 280 SL (Mercedes)." On the night before Valentine's Day he told me to go out to the garage and see my gift. There was my 280 SL! I always said the greatest gift is thinking of others by giving yourself. Rusty certainly out did himself that year!

Our marriage had many storms those first twenty-five years. We experienced unfaithfulness, our son's drug addiction, and living what they call a "married single life." I raised the children and took care of our home while Rusty was very busy with a successful business. Our priorities were different, but we kept on trying to do the best we could.

Right after our twenty-fifth wedding anniversary we separated, and soon filed for a divorce. It took a miracle to work our marriage out. Eight months after we separated Rusty went on a trip to Australia with our son Todd. On a hike up Ayers Rock Rusty made a life-changing decision. He put his faith in God. For twenty-five years I had prayed for him to come to know my Lord. Shortly after he returned home from Australia, we worked to create a new marriage through counseling and courting.

Our courtship the second time around was filled with interesting experiences. One night a mysterious person dressed in an ape suit knocked on my door and handed me a note that said, "Come with me to the Delta King for dinner." I had no idea who this person was and wasn't interested in going out to dinner with a strange ape. I said to him, "Please wait on the porch for a minute," and I called my neighbor who told me to definitely not go! But I decided why not? I needed some adventure in my life. At the restaurant the ape handed me another note saying, "He'd be right back." I sat at the bar waiting for the mysterious big monkey to return thinking to myself, "I must be nuts!" He was still gone when I heard the band start to play, "I Can't Help Falling In Love With You." This was our favorite song before we were married. The ape-man walked up to me and asked me to dance, removing his ape head. It was Rusty after all.

We continued to work hard at our marriage through many hours of prayer and counseling. With God's faithfulness, we renewed our wedding vows on March 9, 1991. Twenty-six years after the first wedding, we were finally united in our determination to keep Christ at the center of our lives. I had dreamed and prayed for this day, the happiest of my life. Our drug-free son walked me down the aisle with our beautiful daughter singing, "Let's Begin Again." I walked toward a totally transformed man. ONLY GOD. For two years and five months we lived a life as only my dreams had imagined. We were happier than we had ever been in our lives. I felt forever grateful for that time.

Little did I know the most difficult time was ahead of us. On August 28, 1993 we were in a motor home accident with our daughter, Nikki. Nikki's body was badly broken. Rusty and I were severely injured with third and fourth degree burns. I had a broken back and was 48% burned. Rusty was 68% burned with only a 9% chance of living.

This was another test of faith in our lives. Had we not grown spiritually from the hard work of rebuilding our marriage, I know we wouldn't have survived this test of fire and the long years of recovery.

Our marriage is truly based on our faith in God and our love for each other. We have made it through the tests, and we wear our scars as a badge of courage.

The Love of My Life

Wonder what my favorite thing is? Even if you don't, I am going to tell you. Actually, I am going to give you a hint! They come in all shapes and sizes, all colors, some loud, some quiet. Give up?

Every since I can remember, I have loved children. At age eleven, when everyone else had Elvis Presley posters on their walls, I had baby pictures from all over the world. I had names for them all and said some day I was going to adopt children from everywhere. My dream became a reality when I started babysitting and collecting kids. My family moved to California when I was thirteen. I went house to house with hand-written posters advertising my babysitting talents. The business poured in. Many times I would care for the kids for nothing just to be with them. As I got older and had so many jobs, I would pick the family with the largest house to be able to baby-sit groups of kids at one time. The parents didn't seem to mind and the kids loved it! At fifty cents an hour per family I made a lot of money in one night. Just think, five dollars for eleven hours!

All I ever wanted was to get married and have eight kids of my own. I wanted little ones I never had to give back at the end of the evening.

When I was pregnant with my first baby Nikki, I was eighteen years old and so excited. I would lie and feel her move inside me, picturing what she would look like. I wanted her to have my coloring with dark hair, the shape of my eyes, and the sky blue eyes of her Daddy.

She finally arrived, and we saw her as the most beautiful bald, blue-eyed baby in the nursery. She never cried but smiled and loved to sleep. I would wake her up just to dress and play with her through the day. Nikki was my little doll forever.

A few years later, our adorable son, Todd, was born. Oh my gosh! What a different baby he was. He was on the go day and night! I was grateful for every ounce of experience and the energy of youth because he kept me moving twenty hours a day. Some days Nikki and I would just stand and watch him run circles around us, not quite sure what to do with him. He had an imagination that was beyond explanation. His little curly head of hair and bright blue eyes charmed everyone he met.

My prayer for eight kids dissolved after three miscarriages. God always knew my love for children, so He started sending kids to our home that needed a place to be loved and nurtured. It's funny how God gives us the desires of our heart, even if it is not the way we planned. When I counted the children in my life there were nine total. That is one more child than I had asked God for.

God is good! Kids have always been a part of my life. Whether my own or other people's, it really did not matter to me. I will always be there to help a child in need.

I now have five wonderful grandchildren of my own and many others who call me "Grandma." To my delight, they are all a huge part of me. They make me laugh, sing and feel alive.

"Thank you Lord for all the children in my life and any others that you want to send my way."

The Reunion

Once again the high school reunion invitation arrived just as it had every five years for the past forty years. I quickly started to call the four friends I was closest to in high school. One by one they had a reason for not attending. I thought to myself, "That is all right, I will have fun anyway. I make friends easily." As the time approached I became apprehensive about attending. I found myself saying, "It is a six hour drive; why am I going?" A new friend in our new town was attending her reunion on the same weekend. She was looking forward to her reunion. What was wrong with me?

I bought a new outfit and had my hair done. I felt pretty and excited about those I would see after such a long period of time. As Rusty and I entered the room, I looked around for a familiar name on a nametag or a face I recognized. I stood at the sign-in table and asked about a few names that I remembered. Each time the person registering me said the person whom I asked about was not coming. "That is all right," I said to myself. "I will just go around and introduce myself." Surely I have to remember someone."

In meeting new people, it dawned on me that who I was in high school was definitely a completely different person than who I am today. It reminded me of how insecure, shy, unpopular, poor, and outcast I felt. I wanted so desperately to belong and be accepted by others. But I was not. There were a few people who remembered me, but I am afraid I did not remember them! Their names sounded familiar, but I had no contact with them while we were in school.

The highlight of the evening was when one gal I didn't recognize said to me, "Sue Arthur, I will always admire you. There you were on graduation night seven months pregnant in your cap and gown all excited about getting your diploma. You were the first one in the gym that night." I was proud of myself for finishing high school, as I was the only married pregnant girl in my class. I made it! I felt proud to say that I am still married to that same wonderful man.

We sat at a table with eight other people. We introduced ourselves but found most of us did not remember many people. As I looked around, I realized that a lot of the same people in school who were popular had grouped up with each other, just as they did way back then. I was richly blessed to be sitting next to two men that were both "nerds" in school. One of their wives had mentioned that it had been a painful time. That statement was probably true for many people around me. As we all talked about our lives now, I felt that I had been placed at that particular table for a reason. Most all of us had been successful in our adult lives no matter how we were accepted during our four years of high school. One man has been a rocket scientist for the past twenty-five years at Edwards Air Force base. The other was an executive for IBM. Many of the others at our table owned their own successful businesses. Those four years of high school were important but just a drop in a bucket of time compared to a lifetime.

As I continued to walk around, one lovely lady and her father remembered me. Actually, they remembered my circumstances. They reminisced about knowing my stepsister and her fiancé, Bob. All were close friends sharing a love of motorcycles and the same church group. They relived the time when a drunk driver killed my sister and badly injured Bob. My sister and her fiancé were one week away from their wedding day.

In a matter of an instant, our lives changed forever. My stepmother blamed my father and divorced him. She quickly left the state during the summer between my junior and senior year. Soon after, my father was committed to a mental institute. I went to live with another family so I could finish at the same high school. The lady and her father told me a lot of details that I did not know or chose to forget. What a sad time in my life. Thank God I had Rusty!

That night we slept in our motor home in the driveway of one of my friends who had chosen not to attend. That next morning as we sat together at breakfast, I told her about the evening. She was a cheerleader with nice clothes. I always thought she was very popular. She wasn't my friend in those days, but rather a friend of my friend. Somehow, we had stayed in touch over the years. I couldn't believe it when she told me that she was popular only because she did what everyone else did, no matter if it was right or wrong. I knew they all drank a lot. Unfortunately, as an adult she became a full-blown alcoholic. That was one of the reasons she did not want to go to the reunion. She figured everyone was still drinking and she did not. The saddest thing was **she never felt popular**. Isn't life interesting?

The Destruction of Suicide

The phone finally rang and my heart stood still as I answered. I was standing in a hotel room in Las Vegas waiting for my sister, Bobby, to pick me up. She was three hours late for our long awaited reunion, and I was starting to get worried about her. My husband and I had arrived the night before for a convention. My sister was very depressed when I called her to make plans for the following day.

I slowly said "Hello." It was my brother-in-law, Jesse. He said quietly, "Your sister is in the hospital. I will be right there to pick you up." As I waited, I kept wondering what went wrong? I knew she had a doctor's appointment that morning to check her and the unborn baby she was carrying. I knew the circumstances of the new baby were confusing. It was not her husband's baby. But he was willing to forgive her and was delighted to finally become a father. For many years they tried without success to have a child of their own. Jesse was in the service overseas for many years. I think my sister's loneliness drove her to have an affair.

On the way to the hospital Jesse had told me that my sister had tried to kill herself. I knew of one other time when she was trying to get attention from our stepmother. I kept remembering her saying to me, "You are always there when I need to laugh." We entered the room and saw tubes like a road map up and down her body and the small lump of the baby. The only sound was of the machine breathing for her. I wanted to scream, "No you didn't have to do this. I am here and I will make you laugh." The doctors told us that too much damage had been done to save either her or the baby. For some reason she had taken an overdose that morning.

Jesse and I sat quietly together waiting. My sister, Bobby, was three years older than me. She was only twenty-nine years old. Our mother died when I was eight and she was eleven. Our father suffered with mental illness. By this time in our lives, we had become familiar with loss.

As we waited, Jesse told me what happened to him while he was stationed overseas in the desert. He had received the "Dear John" letter from my sister. He was in shock and couldn't believe it. He got into his jeep and drove as fast as he could to a place by himself in the desert. Once again he read the dreadful words of rejection and started to tear the letter up into a million pieces. "What the Hell," were his only words. He picked up the gun that was in the seat beside him. With his free hand he threw the million tiny pieces of pain out into the sand. Jesse raised the gun to his head, looked down one more time, and stopped. As he looked, all he could see were the tiny white pieces of paper formed into a cross. He uttered, "God are you really here? Do you have a plan for me?" His gun slowly returned to its place on the seat beside him. Not long after, he returned home with forgiveness in his heart for my sister. Bobby was alone and accepted him back.

Jesse and I prayed together. As we did, my sister slowly left this earth. I had a vision of her in heaven. I could see my sister running into the arms of our mother. Finally she was smiling and laughing. She had never seemed happy after our Mom died, and we were never very close. Now I envied her. I too wished I could be in the arms of my mother. My own life seemed confusing and lonely at this point. I now had to find our mentally ill, homeless father in the streets in San Francisco to tell him his oldest daughter was dead.

I miss having a sister. At times I wish I could have made her laugh more so that she would have wanted to stay with us. I tried to love her unconditionally even though there were many troubled times.

Do you have someone in your life that has committed suicide? Do you say, "If only I would have done this or that, then things could be different?" Many times as I thought about my sister, I realized once again it is my choice. I could choose to carry the guilt from her death and let it turn me into a bitter woman, or I could go on and be the best I can be.

Perhaps your pain is so extreme you are thinking of taking your own life. You feel alone and think no one would care anyway. Your family would be better off without you. Your life is too hard, and you can't make it through another day.

I too have felt that way in my life a few times. The main thing that kept me from suicide was thinking of the people I would leave behind. I asked myself, "Who would care for my children?" or "How would I be remembered?" On those days I would make a goal for myself to achieve. It could be in the next hour, or in a day, or a week. I needed something to look forward to. I prayed for inner strength to see the good in each day. And I did not allow myself to be alone. I asked for help! Don't be resistant to anyone that is trying to help you.

I heard a song by Josh Groham not long ago that said, **"Don't give up, because you want to be heard… Everybody wants to be understood… Everybody wants to be loved."** *("You are Loved*

Don't Give Up") God does understand, He loves you, and He does hear your cry. **Don't give up!**

My Father

I was running out the door when the phone rang. "Hello," I said quickly. The woman on the other end asked, "Is this Susan?" "Yes," I answered. She went on to explain that she worked at a mental health facility in Southern California. She then asked the question I had been waiting to hear for years. "Do you know anyone named Denver?" I stood stunned and almost dropped the phone. I couldn't speak I was so filled with emotion. "That is my father," I answered. He had been living in the streets, and I had not heard a word from him for the past two years. He was now in a safe place where, hopefully, he could get help.

Just that very week my two friends and I started praying for our families. I prayed that the Lord would let me know one way or the other if my father was still alive. Finally, I had an answer. God is good.

My father was diagnosed with paranoid schizophrenia many years before and was able to get help through mental institutions. When the law changed, many of those institutions closed their doors. He lost his job and home ending up living on the streets. All he had was an old broken down car in which he was living.

As I think back to the early days, I remember how my father and his situation helped me make the decision to go to the Woman's Bible Study each week. Every morning my father would wait in his car at the end of our street watching for my husband to go to work. I was very young when my husband, Rusty, and I met. Dad never liked him. As I think back, I realize Dad must have been afraid of Rusty. As soon as Rusty left for work, he would arrive at our house and stay all day. The one good thing about this situation was that I knew he had eaten. The bad thing was that I had a child with ADHD who never stopped moving and needed all my attention. Always good and quiet, my little girl was three years older than her brother. Her needs were totally overwhelmed by her brother's. Now my father was pulling me away as well.

Now add to this chaos my father who changed his moods every few minutes. I will never forget the day that Dad asked, "Can I have a pair of scissors to trim my hair." Without thinking I gave him scissors and walked away. A few minutes later he angrily stood in front of me holding the scissors like a knife pointed right at me. I was scared, and I realized we were all in danger on a regular basis. I had to watch him like a hawk. I felt like I was going to go crazy!

Knowing my situation, a friend asked me if I would like to go with her to Bible Study Fellowship. At first I said, "No I don't need that." I was twenty-three years old and thought I had it all together. What a joke! My friend kept asking me. Finally, she told me, "They have childcare and you can have a few hours away from your Dad." BINGO! That did it.

From that point on, I never missed a week. Dad would follow me to the church and wait for me until I finished. I had three hours once a week just for myself In the beginning, I was so exhausted that the ladies just let me sleep. I met women in my small group that would listen to me and pray with me for help for my father and safety for my family. Within a few weeks God supplied answers helping me respond to Dad in the correct way. I couldn't change him, but I could change how I responded. Many times I would argue with Dad when he said crazy things. I would try to talk him out of what he was saying and correct him. It only made him madder. You see, in his state of mind what he was saying was true to him. Most importantly, Bible Study Fellowship taught me how to have a personal relationship with my HEAVENLY FATHER, which was my salvation.

A year after I started Bible Study, we moved to the country. With Dad's limited funds, it was too far for him to drive back and forth. He was dangerous at times; so one side of me felt relief and the other side felt guilt. With this move, my father had to change his regular routine. The move was a blessing in disguise. I was finally able to get help from a social worker for him. She found him a care home. As long as he took his pills, he did well. The hard part was keeping him on the medications he needed to stay sane. Unfortunately, that arrangement did not last long.

Before I knew it, Dad was on the streets in San Francisco. It is hard to explain the pain I felt when I got a collect call from him. He was cold, hungry, and alone with nowhere to go. He would put newspaper underneath his worn-out jacket to stay warm, hiding in the shelter of the doorway of the library at night. He ate at St. Anthony Hall one meal a day. As I sat in my warm house, the feelings of guilt would rush over me. Every time I opened the refrigerator I wanted to be sick. How can I help someone so mentally ill? There did not seem to be any answers, and I felt so helpless.

To add to my feelings of helplessness, my husband and I were living a single married life. There was not much communication between us. He did his thing and I did mine. I was so young I believed this was a normal way of life. I did not have anyone with whom to talk. Matter of fact, I don't even remember talking to my husband, Rusty, about my father or giving him a chance to help me.

Many times Dad tried to jump from the Golden Gate Bridge. When the police stopped him, they would call me. We lived an hour and a half away from the city, so by the time I got there, my father was always gone because he refused help. I walked through the streets my father described on the phone without finding him. I watched all the other lost souls with nowhere to go. It was hard to picture my father in this place.

After so much time had passed without contact, I became desperate to find him. Every time there was a news report saying, "Man found in park unidentified," I would call to get information. Several times I drove down to the morgue and looked at the bodies. I felt such fear overcome me. How can there be so many lost people? I didn't want to see the reality of that lifestyle. I wanted to be sheltered from it. Now, for some reason, I was living in the middle of it. I soon realized this could happen to anyone of us. I was so grateful I had my Heavenly Father with me to give me the strength I needed for that time in my life.

Finally, after years of living this nightmare, my prayers were being answered. I listened to the woman on the other end of the phone tell me about my father and his condition. A sense of thankfulness overcame me. I finally knew where my father was. He had care in that institution until he died.

Do any of you know someone like my father? I know at times the situation seems hopeless, but my only answer was to rely on the Lord and to find care for my father. I couldn't do anything for him myself.

I saw this powerful answer to prayer. Living this journey with my father has given me the gift of compassion for lost souls. I always knew my father LOVED me, and I knew mental illness was not WHO my father was.

The Look of Deception

What does a young woman look like when she is suffering from so much loss and feeling empty? I was looking at some old picture albums today. It was the day after Christmas with gray clouds and a chill in the air. As I turned each page, I could see years of time and experiences that our family had shared. There were many Christmases pictured in those pages. The children have all grown, and so have my husband and I.

In every picture I looked at closely, I saw a pretty young girl without lines on her face with a beautiful smile. She always seemed to be happy and had a much smaller frame than she has today. I was that girl.

One particular picture caught my eye. As I studied it, I remembered back to the day it was taken. Anyone would have thought this young beautiful, thin, well-dressed, twenty-seven year-old with long dark hair had it all together. I do have to say I was pretty cute! It is too bad that I didn't appreciate and believe in myself back then. The day that picture was taken was a very sad day for me. I remember my husband planning an overnight trip to San Francisco to stay at the new Hyatt Regency hotel. I kept saying to myself, "I am too upset to go," However, Rusty insisted, so we went.

Just a few weeks prior to this trip, my father-in-law and best friend, had died suddenly. Exactly two weeks before his death, my only sister had committed suicide. One of the saddest parts of her death was that I could not find our homeless father to tell him of his daughter's death. I knew my father was in San Francisco somewhere.

He lived on the street and was impossible to find. On this overnight to the Hyatt I had nothing to celebrate.

When we finally arrived at the hotel, a miracle happened. We had just gotten out of the car parked under the overhang. As I stood on the curb waiting for the attendant to give us the parking ticket, I glanced across the street. I could see a small, short man with blue eyes and black hair. He was dressed in a torn old suit with a dirty white shirt and a tie. I knew immediately that it was my father. He started to walk towards me and I him. We held onto each other sobbing. I blurted, "Daddy I love you." He repeated, "I love you too!" Without giving me a chance to give him the horrid news about my sister Bobby's suicide, he turned and walked away. Paralyzed, I let him go. I still feel much pain when I think about my father. Having a loved one that is mentally unbalanced and homeless often feels like a hopeless situation.

So you see how deceptive that photo of the well-dressed young wife was? Sometimes the truth is **behind** the picture **not in** it. I don't think I believe that pictures tell a thousand words. At least that one didn't. What is it that every photographer says before he or she takes a picture? SMILE. They don't ask you to look like you might feel. Half the time when I was young, I didn't know how I felt. My attitude depended on other people's moods. I wanted to make everyone happy so that they would like me. I am so grateful today as I look back on the stages of my life, that my main man is God my Savior. Without Him, I would not have made the decisions I did to help me through the tough times of my life.

Life is full of decisions, and I could have traveled a much different path than God chose for me. I was so insecure, and I had no self worth when I was young. Seven immediate members of my family were dead by the time I was twenty-six. I learned at an early age that God would never leave me. Everyone that was living did. My greatest fear was that my husband and children would die. I depended on God because He said He would never forsake me.

My picture albums helped me realize how much a life can change. When we are young, our appearance is so important. We think it will make us happy. As we grow older, it might be marriage and children that will make us complete. Then we get to a stage where we wish we had more money and a big house. And life goes on and on. More than fifty years have come and gone in my life. Now I know after all these years what God has been telling me all along - **self-worth is the key**. He always knew how special I was. It just took me a while to figure this out. It is not any of those outside components. You can never be too shapely or have enough money to make you happy. Christ is the only perfect One around! But get this - **We are made in His image!**

Chapter Two

Growing Through Adversity

> *I thank God for turning my world upside down because it forced me to change. Out of struggle comes beauty.*

What Was Your Name?

I looked over at the man sleeping next to me. He was all cuddled up snoring softly with his light brown hair tossed back to show his handsome face. It was very early in the morning, and my mind was racing with doubts of my future.

We had been married for many years, but I still did not have the security I needed. We were married right out of high school when I was eighteen and started a family immediately. My husband was older. He worked in his own business eighteen hours a day, seven days a week for the first ten years. My life was the children. His life was business. Our children were now teenagers, and I knew it would not be long until they were gone.

As I looked at my husband sleeping, I kept thinking, "Who are you?" We had been together for nine months before our daughter was born. Now, if we were lucky, we'd have the kids around only another five years. Then what? I felt as if I were lying next to a stranger, unsure of our future together. All I knew was how to raise kids. Sure, they were a lot of work and we had many challenging times. But our home was filled with much laughter and fun. Would I ever have fun again once they were gone? I hardly knew this man! We had such different lives even though we shared the same home and family.

That was the morning the light bulb went on in my head. I was determined not to wake up when I was forty-something and say, "What was your name?" and "What am I going to do now?"

I started to prepare for the empty nest. Our youngest was fourteen, and I no longer had to work in his classroom. He was ADHD, and his teachers insisted I volunteer two days a week while he was in the lower grades. He consumed most of my time and energy. Now, I finally had some time of my own to think about what I wanted to do.

The fall semester was starting at the junior college near my home. I had always been interested in interior design. With education in that field, I could possibly work in my husband's construction company.

When I started taking classes, I felt like a young girl again. At the same time it felt strange doing something just for myself. Everyone at home still needed me, but I found it was important for me to have an interest of my own.

In our house on a wall between our two children's room hung a parent's prayer. I read it often while the children were growing up. It was a constant reminder that our children are not our own. When I prayed for them, I would always start my prayer by thanking God for loaning me His children to raise for Him. What an awesome responsibility. In the tough times I would question, "Are you sure Lord you sent me the right kids?" Then I would remember the verse that says, *"God will not allow any difficulty to come into our lives that we are not capable of bearing"* (1 Corinthians 10:13 my version). Also, *"Train up a child in the way he should go, And when he is old he will not depart from it"* Proverbs 22:6, NKJ. I was always grateful for the Lord's confidence in me and the encouragement I got from His Word.

Struggling through each teenage conflict, I realized that the kids were no longer the highlight of my life. With each incident, I would realize that their rebellion was one more way of breaking away from home. It all started to make sense.

You see, when they were cute little babies, they needed us to take care of them. We loved being with them. Then, we had years of teaching and molding to hopefully build the perseverance and character for them to learn to make the right choices. By the time they were teenagers wanting to try their own wings, they were not very pleasant to be around. It was all part of God's plan.

I trusted God to help me raise His kids. My question at the time of their departure was, "Do I trust Him enough to care for them night and day when they are on their own?"

Did I doubt God or myself on the job I did in raising them? I knew I did the best job I could. So I needed to trust my kids and my God to show me. Of course, there were mistakes made. But haven't we all fallen down once in a while?

Our daughter took Plan A. She was graduated, went on to college, and did very well on her own. I was always so proud of her. When she left, I missed her smiling face and agreeable attitude.

Our son picked Plan D. This plan was one that I prayed no one else has to go through. He chose to be kicked out of our home because of a drug addiction. The smiling little boy that once took all my time and attention was on his own now in a very scary world. My heart was broken yet my trust in God was constant. My knees were ruby red from all my prayers for him.

My handsome husband awakened to a situation on which we both had to work together. Working together was new to us, but we had to make decisions together and stick to them. Those five years battling our son's drug addiction were some of the most difficult years of our lives. At times I wondered how we lived through them. I realize the guidance we got in the early years played a large role in our survival. My husband and I grew closer. Our son was forced to detach from us and run to the only arms that were open to him. Guess whose arms those were? God's! This is definitely not the way I would have chosen to have an empty nest.

I remembered the verse, *"Train up a child in the way he should go, And when he is old he will not depart from it"* Proverbs 22:6, NKJ. Now I know that they can go away for a little while, but they will return. Our son fought the battle of drugs, and God delivered him completely. He went onto Bible College and is a pastor who works with young people. I had always prayed for him to serve the Lord. Little did I know during the dark times how bright our future would become.

I was always grateful for the Lord's guidance and wisdom. I finally realized His chain of command: first in our lives is God, second are our husbands, and third are our children. As a mother I somehow got it all mixed up. My husband and I lived married single lives. He did his thing and I did mine to the point of not knowing each other. I was consumed with being a mother and made our kids my whole world. Where else did my husband have to go but work?

I believed finding an outside interest would do me a world of good. Not only did I get an education that gave me self-esteem, it also made me a more interesting person. I learned respect earns respect.

Our family has always stayed close. After several years, we all made a decision to move back together again. Our children and their families, along with my husband and I, moved to a large ranch. Our houses were side by side. All ten of us worked together raising kids and animals. God is GOOD and we are truly BLESSED.

Empty Nest

There are a lot of ways for your children to leave home. The best way is for them to grow, become independent, go off to college, and learn to be responsible for themselves. I was always told a mother's job was to give their children roots and wings. Many mothers dread the day the kids grow up and leave.

For our family, our first child did just that. Nikki was what I call an "easy keeper". She had a few problems in her teens, but we all looked forward to who she would become as a grown woman.

Unfortunately, our son was both a blessing and a challenge. Todd was diagnosed with Attention Deficit Hyperactivity Disorder (ADHD) as a very young child. From age two until six, the doctors tried to get me to approve giving him the drug Ritalin. I always refused. After being kicked out of four nursery schools, Bible Study Fellowship, and Sunday school, we decided we needed to do something. With much prayer and good advice from our son's pre-first grade teacher, we went through a series of tests at the University of California at San Francisco.

Todd was six years old and closely monitored while on the drug. I was so afraid of what Ritalin might do to him that I only gave it to him during school for six hours a day. He had none after school, on weekends, or during summer vacations. I wanted him to know how to handle himself without medication. He was on Ritalin for three years. Then, we discontinued it completely.

Life was not easy in the following years, but Todd made it through school until his senior year. His behavior started to change and we realized he was self-medicating with the amphetamine, Speed. Ritalin and Speed affected Todd the same way. After seeking help at a drug rehab center, I was told 75% of children admitted had been on some drug as a young child. That was back in 1987. I can't imagine what the numbers are now.

Finally my husband told our eighteen-year-old son, "Stop using and go to school, or you need to move out." My heart stopped when I watched him pack his bags and go out the front door.

I knew we had to do something to help Todd. We had been the best parents we knew how to be, but now his choices were up to him. He was of legal age. His habit grew to a hundred dollars a day. Many of our processions were missing, and the creditors called about bad checks. It was hard to believe this was happening to our family. For a long time I did not know where Todd was. As I looked at our picture wall, I would weep at his loss as I looked at how he used to be. What happened to this happy curly-haired little boy so full of energy? Each night I would lie in bed wondering if he was dead or alive. I tried to prepare for the empty nest, but there is no way a parent can prepare for this loss.

Often I would second-guess our decision. Down deep I knew it was the right one. Our son had to learn to pay the consequence for his actions. We had always been there for him and supported him in all that he did. There was never any doubt that we loved our youngest child, and he always knew that. But supporting and loving him was not enough, he was still a drug addict.

Family drug counseling taught me that what we had always done was not working. I needed to change my reactions to his actions. It would force him to change. So I reversed my actions. "Tough love" is what we called it. And it is not easy to do! I think as parents, we are always afraid our children will think we do not love them. By reversing our reactions we are showing we love them even more. Besides, they know down deep we love them.

Luckily, we did not have younger children in our family. Our daughter was three years older. Nikki quickly grew sick of her brother bringing so much pain into our family. He always got all the attention, good or bad. This made her feel left out most of her young life.

Now as I watch families travel this same road, I feel their pain and loss. I watch the other children being left out. These other children dread visits or phone calls from their out-of-control sibling because he/she corrupts the entire household. These other children are left screaming or crying in frustration at their sibling. Their needs and wants are pushed to the back as the sibling on drugs drains everyone in a spiraling cycle of chaos. Their sister or brother has been taken over by a drug making him or her into someone they do not like or know. Will this HELL ever end? I am sure, just like my daughter, they wonder why we put up with so much. I know in my case, I just kept praying that all his lies about changing would be true and maybe this time it would be different.

It was never different until we changed ourselves. We had to let him make his own choices. We had to DO THE OPPOSITE OF WHAT WE ALWAYS DID. Our way of responding changed, so his actions changed also. It still took time and there were a lot of sleepless

58

nights, but something changed in us. We could go on with our lives without the fear of feeling the drug had control of our family. It helped me to remember the drug might still have control of my child but his actions are the drug talking, not the child we raised.

I always hung onto the verse, *"Train up a child in the way he should go, and when he is old he will not depart from it"* Proverbs 22:6, NKJ. My version is, "He might go away for a little while, but he will return." Thank God He is good to His word. My son is now a pastor of his own church.

My prayers are with families who are going through your own journey now. Keep praying for God's wisdom, grace, and guidance to help you through.

The Heartbreak of Drug Abuse

"You are no longer our son, and you are not welcome in our home anymore." I heard those words come out of my husband's mouth early one morning. I felt like someone had taken a knife and stabbed me in the heart. One side of me wanted to protect my youngest child. The other side was angry with my husband for saying such harsh words. I was not ready to let go of my only son. I had always made my children my life. I had tried to prepare for the empty nest when the time arrived. But nothing could prepare me for this time in our lives.

We had been in this incredibly painful process for two years. The three of us had gone through an eight-week outpatient drug therapy. At least my husband and I had. We all began the program together, but our son had dropped out early. My husband and I agreed that we would finish it no matter what our son chose to do. During those sessions we learned some tools to help us through this never-ending hell.

Al Anon came next and then finally a sixty-day inpatient program. We seemed to be taking one step at a time to try to help him and ourselves. The one thing parents always need to remember is that a substance has taken over their child. No matter how hard you try, you can't control it. Most of the time they cannot either. They have to want this horrible journey to end as much as you do.

On this fateful rainy morning our son Todd had only been out of the drug center two days. After his release, we put him in a halfway house where he was told, "If you use or don't follow the rules, you will be kicked out. No second chances." In the wee hours of the morning, we received a call from the halfway house letting us know our son had been caught using drugs again and was out of the program. I recall both of us crying and lying in our bed. We were each in our own quiet hell not knowing what to do next. We were grateful for all the counseling we had received during both programs. The main thing we learned was that we had to stick together in whatever decision we made. Once more we had to do something.

Now as my husband opened the door to our son, I heard those awful words come out of his mouth. He said them quietly with much disappointment. I wanted to scream, "Wait! We haven't talked about this yet!" But in my soul, I knew he was right. This hell had to end for all of our sakes. We had tried everything and the Lord had guided us to the help we had received. But now, we had to turn our son completely over to the grace of God. I kissed him goodbye and watched him walk away wondering if I would ever see him again.

This energetic little boy with his curly hair and happy smile who I had spent so much time raising was gone. I was grateful he was over eighteen, but the pain was like losing a child to death. Each time I went down the hallway of our house filled with photos, I was reminded of much happier times in our lives. I mourned over his loss when I studied his face in those pictures, and I would weep until no tears were left.

Drug addiction affects each family member differently. Our older daughter was angry with her brother. Todd was ADHD and had always demanded all our attention, time, and energy. She had been the forgotten child. Once again she could see the pain he was creating. Being away at school, she worried for our safety, horrified with what could happen. The drug dealers knew where we lived. Many of our processions were stolen to support his habit. This was an unknown world to us. We had only heard about it before, but now we were living in it.

Days and months passed without any contact. We prayed and prayed, going through the motions of daily life. I went over and over in my head what we had learned through the process of treatments and attended *Al Anon* meeting for support. I had to remind myself of the important things we'd learned:

Do not allow the, "IF ONLY" to take over your thinking. I know we did the best we could for our son while raising him. NO GUILT TRIPS! It doesn't help anyone. You did the best you knew how.

Make a decision and stick by it! If you say no living in this house while you are using, MEAN IT.

Parents need to support each other. Don't be slipping the kid a twenty-dollar bill in his pocket while he's walking out the door. You might worry about him not eating, but he won't use it for food anyway.

This is not the child you raised. The words out of his or her mouth and their actions are the DRUGS talking. Be angry with that.

Know, "You cannot control this DRUG, it is too big."

If what you have tried does not work, DO THE OPPOSITE.

PRAY and turn them over. Something has stolen your child, and you cannot stop it.

We had such good advice and I will never forget it. I will always remember the example of the Pillow Story.

You have this adorable baby, and you meet his needs and protect him from harm. While he is learning to walk, you throw a pillow down in front of him so he doesn't get hurt. They learn to ride a bike and you still have that pillow. The question is, "When do we stop wanting to help our children not feel the pain of the fall?" This story made so much sense to me. It is all about teaching our kids to take responsibility and pay the consequence for their own actions so they do not want or need to numb the pain of their lives with drugs. Do the drugs replace the pillow?

Not all stories have a happy ending, but our DOES. God has blessed our family by keeping our son alive. He protected Todd when I could not. We had a very long five years coping with drug abuse. By the grace of God, He totally took our son and turned him around. I feel a drug-addicted person is living in a journey of hell. Our son yelled out for God to save him from that hell. God answered him and delivered him from the addiction. He gave Todd a heart to serve the Lord, and now our son is a pastor working with young people from all walks of life. He has a beautiful wife and four adorable children.

I had always believed the verse, *"Train up a child in the way he should go, and when he is old he will not depart from it"* Proverbs 22:6, NKJ. I claimed this verse, but now I say to others it does not say, "He might leave for a little while, but he will return."

First published in "Good News Northwest" February 2007.

Choices To Make Me Grow

Have you ever thought back to the choices you have made? How have they directed your life? How have they driven you to where you are now?

In the wee hours of the morning, my husband Rusty awakened me from a sound sleep. Still groggy I heard him say, "We need to talk!" That grabbed me because we rarely did. We were ages twenty-six and thirty-three and living married single lives. I was raising children, while he was building his business. "I am not happy, and I want a divorce," he announced. "I love you, but I am not in love with you. There is someone else." He also said he would like to stay until after Christmas, which was soon. Then he added, "By the way, I am going duck hunting tomorrow."

I laid in shock not knowing whether to scream, cry or just kill myself. I felt rejected and unloved. I begged him not to leave me. I would do anything he wanted to make myself good enough. One side of me felt desperate; the other was just pathetic. Rusty was the only man in my life since I was fifteen. I couldn't believe that I would now be left alone to raise our two small children. I had never worked. My mom was dead, and my mentally ill father was living somewhere on the streets. My only sister committed suicide. I was totally alone. My biggest fear was coming true. Being left behind usually came to me through death, not by choice. I lay awake not wanting to believe what I had just heard.

When morning light appeared, it seemed just a nightmare. Everything and everyone went on as usual. As soon as I was alone, I called my pastor. He came and talked to me for hours. I felt I needed to get out of there and think. Since my husband was off hunting ducks for the first time, I made arrangements for the kids, and called my sister-in-law, Vincy. Even though she was my husband's sister, she was the only family I had. "How sad," I thought as I hung up! We made arrangements to take a drive to Tahoe.

It was late in the evening before we left during the biggest snowstorm I had ever seen. About half way there, I started to doubt whether I was doing the right thing. I was feeling sick! I had a strong faith and had prayed with my sister-in-law before we left the house. By the time we arrived in Tahoe, it was four in the morning. As I pulled up to our condo, I saw my husband's truck. "OH MY GOD!" I SCREAMED! Vincy kept saying, "What are we going to do?" All I remember is driving around the block praying for God to guide me and to take over because I DIDN'T KNOW WHAT TO DO.

God's guidance came in a surprising cadence as we finally knocked on our condo door. As Rusty opened the door, I calmly chuckled, "It is too cold for ducks up here!" God has a sense of humor even in the tough times. We walked into the living room where the new girlfriend was sleeping. I looked at her, and then at him. Again, I could hear my voice say, "This is not fair for her, the children, or me. You need to go home and get your stuff. Leave now before Christmas." I was calm and did not shed a tear while I slowly gathered my ski gear out of the closet. I collected my sister-in- law, who had almost fallen down the stairs in shock, and left.

We drove to the nearest motel and checked in. There I had an awakening! I had read in the Bible about the guidance of God, and now I was able to see His power up close and personal. I lay on the bed and shook as I thought back to what had just happened. Was that me? Did I say that? I had asked for God to take over and He had. God had a sense of humor, I realized. He also had compassion for the other gal by thinking of her first. WOW! It was an awful situation. I called my pastor and told him what had just happened.

I was determined to stay there a couple of days, so I was up the mountain skiing first thing the next morning, snowstorm and all. I know I was in shock and felt numb even with the cold. Vincy stayed in the ski-lodge bar and was waiting for me when I came in. She was warm with liquid heat along with a lot of men doing the same. They all seemed to know what happened the night before and were telling me their own stories of woe. We were invited by one of the thirty-something guys to come to a party at his house that was right around the corner from where we were staying. I didn't want to go, but Vincy did. I tried drinking once when I was very young, and it was not a good experience. It made me sadder than I had been already, and I made a decision then that I did not want to ever drink again.

As we entered the man's upstairs apartment, the colorful strobe light of the 60's and 70's filled the room. Everyone was talking, drinking and doing a few drugs. It reminded me of eighteen year olds. I had prayed before I went because I was scared. I had never been brave when it came to men or parties, and I felt very insecure. I knew I was vulnerable. I had to choose to be responsible for the sake of the kids. I also knew I was the only one to care for them. I quickly got an unopened can of seven-up and carried it around with me. I kept thinking someone could drug me. So many men were paying attention to me. I liked being the one sought after, but as I watched, I kept saying, "I don't want to end up like all of these lost souls." Vincy was having a good time as the conversation about the night before continued. Every time someone new came in, it was repeated once again. I was a star! Little did they know I had nothing to do with it. My star twinkled because of God's light. I watched all that was going on around and thought, "How sad."

All these wonderful people had made choices in their own difficult circumstances. They had been hurt and chose to numb their pain. They were stuck!

As we drove home the next day, I continued to thank God for His intervention, and for the hard lessons I had learned that weekend. It did not change my circumstances, but it did change me. It gave me more confidence in myself because it gave me confidence in God. I wanted Him to be in control of my life!

As I think back to that story, I remember being so afraid of being alone. I cried many tears through the difficult days. I am so glad I had my faith to fall back on when I could no longer rely on my husband to care for me.

Desires of Your Heart

"We trust as we love and where we love. If we love Christ much,
truly we shall trust Him much."

Thomas Brooks

It was late at night in front of my house. The floodlights were on, and worship music was playing in the background. I sat in the dirt beside four flats of flowers waiting to be planted. Tears rolled down my cheeks as I thought back over the past twenty-five years. I had married this man when I was eighteen years old, and now he wanted a divorce. He had just moved his belongings out that day. I was determined to make myself happy by planting my flowers. When I was a child my aunt had always told me that if you have lots of flowers outside your home, it meant you had a happy home. For the first time in my forty-four years, I was totally alone. The children were grown and on their own. Now I was too.

In my early twenties, I realized I needed to be dependent on the Lord instead of my husband. Through the following years he was a workaholic and unfaithful in our marriage. I had struggled to make this wonderful provider happy. I doubled my efforts in being the best I could be. Every day I prayed for God's guidance and wisdom for our family. I knew the only one I could change was myself. I prayed daily for my husband to find God's salvation. I read Psalms 37:4, *"Delight yourself in the Lord and he will give you the desires of your heart."* My desires were to have a family and a husband that loved and adored me. It did not seem to be working out that way, but I hung onto that promise.

Times looked bleak as my husband and I managed to get through some very difficult years by the grace of God. We lived through our son's battles with attention deficit hyperactivity disorder (ADHD) and drug addiction, our daughter's depression, and our own inner battles with each other.

Now I was sitting in the dirt crying as I remembered back. I knew I would be all right by myself because I was not really alone. I had built a relationship with God and He did love me.

It was a difficult time, but I started looking forward to what God had planned for me. It became very exciting - and a relief - to have only myself to consider. I still prayed for my Rusty every day, but soon realized he had to find his own way. The divorce was in place and the clock was ticking. I joined a Christian singles group and attended a divorce recovery workshop. I had gone on with my life and just signed up for college when I got the call.

It was my husband, Rusty. He was on his way over to tell me something. There he stood on the front porch with tears in his eyes, announcing his acceptance of the Lord. He no longer sought a divorce and wanted to work on our marriage. It had been six months since he had left. To be truthful, I doubted whether I even wanted to be married now. Single life was good, fun, and exciting. I was more content than I ever remembered being Did I want to go back to the distrust and deception I had endured for so many years?

My answer to him was, "I need time." I separated myself from the single activities I was involved with and took time to be alone to pray. The Psalmist promised the Lord would give me the desires of my heart when I sought Him first. I had prayed for my husband for twenty-five years to come to know the Lord. Now Rusty said he had. I did not trust my husband, but I did trust God. I realized if I chose not to work to save this marriage, I would doubt God's power and grace the rest of my life.

My husband and I set up personal boundaries and had a lot of Christian counseling. We continued to live alone. As the months went by, God did the work of mending a very broken relationship. As I learned to know my husband and trust him, we fell in love again. For the first time, Christ became the center of our marriage. We renewed our wedding vows in our church on our twenty-sixth wedding anniversary with many friends and family in attendance. It was the happiest day of my life. Our beautiful daughter sang, "Let's Begin Again" and our drug-free son walked me down the aisle to meet a completely transformed man. All my childhood dreams had come true, and I did receive the desires of my heart.

First published in "Chicken Soup for the Christian Woman's Soul" 2002. Reprinted in "Chicken Soup for the Soul – Happily Ever After" 2008.

A Gift for a Season

The other day I received a phone call from someone that was in my life many years ago. It had been at least a dozen years since I had last spoke to him. We laughed and caught up on our families. It was easy to talk about how our lives had been and share a few special memories of the past. After an hour and a half, we reluctantly hung up. It was as if we were both wondering when the next time would be when we would talk again.

As I thought about our conversation, it took me back to the painful time when we first met. After being married for twenty-five years to the husband of my youth, we were getting a divorce. During those years there had been much laughter and many tears. But now it was ending. I had finally given up all hope that my marriage could be saved. The children were grown and now I could go on to work on the second half of my life. After all, I was only forty-four years old.

I had joined a local Christian singles group for the summer. We went together on campouts once a month. This was a new group of people that shared the love of life, faith, and living. I met a neat gal named Sharon who loved to have fun and laugh. That was just what I needed. I remember saying to her, "We need to get together and do some things. We seem to have so much in common." Her response was, "I am going on a trip, but I will call when I return." Suddenly I thought, so am I! I couldn't believe it when she told me she was going on the same singles cruise I was. Only God, can make those plans!

Even with the sad circumstances of my life, I went on through the summer having fun and meeting new people. Two guys from our group joined the fun - Terry and Ric. We did everything as a foursome. I felt safe and happy. I had set boundaries for my relationships. I was available to be a good friend, but my divorce was not complete. I would not cross that boundary. We all traveled together, but I paid my own way, had my own room, and, "DON'T try to kiss me," I would say! Terry loved to go to movies while Ric loved to ride bikes and hike. It was perfect for me. I had friends with whom to play. This was truly what I needed in this time of my life, and God supplied the special people. Life does go on after divorce.

Ric and I did seem to connect but still no kissing. We did a lot of talking, sharing, and laughing. We could talk about anything together. We shared our hidden desires as we looked at each other with smiling eyes. For the first time in my life, I had someone who seemed to be able to read my thoughts and really cared about me.

I had been with my husband since I was fifteen years old. I had never known or even dated another man. He was seven years older and very serious about succeeding in his business. I always felt very low on his priority list. Actually, I was frightened of most men and did not trust them.

God does know just what we all need in our lives. The Lord had become my husband, and I depended on Him for every move and decision I made during that time of being alone. I did trust my Lord to help me through this season.

For eight months I was alone, working on myself, building new relationships, making my own choices and decisions. Then my life once again changed. My husband, Rusty, declared he was now a believer and wanted to work on the marriage. By now Ric was a BIG part of my life. I had made plans to go back to school. I had confidence and good self-esteem for the first time.

I believe that working again on my marriage was one of the hardest decisions I have ever made. I felt I had worked on it alone for the first twenty-five years, and I did not want to do that again. Rusty assured me that he would work very hard to make this marriage work. So I agreed to try for three months. My conditions were: live separately, go to counseling, go to church, and start dating and getting to know each other. If he truly accepted the Lord, Rusty was a new person I needed to know. No kissing was allowed.

As for my new friends, and of course Ric, I had to say goodbye. I could not work on marriage and live a single life too. It was very difficult and we cried many tears. Ric and I stood on my front porch, held each other, and prayed that the Lord's will be done in both of our lives. We kissed for the first and last time. It seemed time stood still.

God had given me the gift of Ric to encourage me, build me up, and fill me with His strength, and show me that I am lovable and a good woman. I needed that. God used Ric to show me that ALL things are possible.

My Lord took a shattered marriage and rebuilt it into a wonderful witness that He can heal broken hearts, mend memories, and offer forgiveness. Even though it was very hard, I will never regret working once again on our marriage. He used my new friends to help me through a very challenging time. Ric was my mentor for that season, and I will be forever grateful to him. He respected me enough to leave me alone during those three months to work on my marriage.

Every now and then he will call just to check on how things are doing. We hang onto each other's words, and know that we did the right thing. Meeting changed both of our lives, and we feel honored to have known each other for a season.

My Spiritual Mom

When I think of my Spiritual Mom I think of the word "mentor". In Webster's dictionary the definition is, *"A person looked upon for wise advice and guidance."*

Our journey began in our neighborhood in Sacramento. I knew of Beryl for quite some time, but felt that we really connected in 1990. I had been without my own mother for forty-three years. As I watched this lovely lady, she mirrored an image of the woman I would love to become. She was full of joy and faith in God that was contagious. She raised four kids of her own with a husband who did not share in her faith at that time.

My life had been full of challenges and my faith had already been tested many times. Our daughter was away at college and our son was struggling with drug addiction. My husband and I had just celebrated our twenty-fifth wedding anniversary when he decided he wanted to end the marriage, and start a new life with someone else.

I remember the day that Beryl and I met at the garden club meeting in the neighborhood. After much prayer, I had decided that I needed to start a life of my own, meet new people, and get involved in activities just for myself. Beryl was attending a church that I had gone to a few times. I knew I needed a Bible study on a daily basis, but was too undisciplined to do it on my own.

This particular day I just said a few words to Beryl that I remember. I needed to tell someone that my husband had just moved out. She looked shocked. I don't recall crying as I told her. I'd already cried so much. I wasn't quite sure what to do. Divorce was something I had feared all my life, and now it was happening to me. Beryl folded me in her arms and said, "It will be all right." Most people heard those words often, but I longed for them. It was what I needed to hear just then.

My connection to her was instant. We began a neighborhood Bible study at my house with seven women once a week. These women became the family that I had never had. They helped me learn to live on my own for the first time in my life. My son Todd was in the army. My daughter Nikki was away at college. That was not an easy time in my life, but God chose these special people to walk through it with me.

Beryl and her husband Art became my guardian angels. They made me feel protected from the scary world around me. I think I ran every decision by them. Art was a lawyer so he checked out the divorce papers for me. We sat at their kitchen table and picked out my room on a singles cruise I decided to take on my own. They heard about every "singles" meeting I attended. I needed to make new friends, both men and women. Since I was only fifteen when I met my husband, I never had any experience meeting other men. It was all pretty scary!

After eight months of being alone, Rusty decided he wanted to be married again. Beryl was there for me in my confusion. Her guidance and prayers helped me in the transition from being a godly single woman to being an obedient wife.

The hard part was I no longer wanted to be married to Rusty anymore. I enjoyed the single life I had made for myself. In her firm Mom voice Beryl would say, "God hates divorce." I knew I had to be obedient to God and trust He would change the desires of my heart. Beryl knew her Bible inside and out. She guided me to God's promises to stand on through that time. The Bible study girls would pray for me as we went through many months of counseling to rebuild our very broken marriage.

As God began putting our marriage back together, Rusty and I began dating each other all over again. One particular night I called Beryl with the question, "Should I go to dinner with a giant ape at my front door with a balloon and note? He asked me to go to the Delta King for dinner." There was silence at the other end of the phone, then a yell, "ART...." I quickly said, "I am going and will call you as soon as I get there. If I don't return you can get fingerprints off the balloon on the kitchen table." The old Rusty would have never done anything like that in the past and I did not know he was in the ape suit!

On March 9, 1991 all my Bible study girls were there to celebrate the most beautiful answer to prayer - our wedding! I could never have dreamt that Rusty and I would be joined in marriage again. We renewed our vows in our church standing side by side with each other and the Lord. Our lives seemed perfect until two years and five months later.

August 28,1993 we were in a near-fatal motor home accident. Once again, Beryl and the girls prayed daily for us. As I think back to those times, they must of gotten tired of praying for me over and over. Times once again were hard not knowing whether we would live or die.

Even through the pain and medications, I knew I needed to hear Beryl's voice. By the power of the Holy Spirit, I was able to tell the nurse her phone number.

Beryl always made me feel it would be OK. At this time in my life I needed to know that. Rusty only had a 9% chance of living. We were not sure if I would ever walk again. Beryl was there to feed me (when the nurses weren't looking). I could count on her to always be standing by me when I needed her. It was a difficult time for all of us. I am sure it was hard for her to look at burned skin and listen to me cry in such sorrow and pain. She made me her famous minestrone soup for my first dinner home from the hospital after two long months. Unfortunately, I threw it up not long after I ate it. The recovery was long and hard. But by the grace of God, and the prayers of all my neighborhood Bible Study girls, we made it through. Many hours, days, and months passed and they all supported and encouraged me all along the way.

Beryl, I will be forever grateful for your love and care. Even though there is distance between us, I feel your presence. I can hear your pride and encouragement each time I call to tell you about another successful story published or speaking engagement I have. Through the years, we have watched God's answers to prayer in both of our lives. Now both of our husbands have accepted Jesus and joined us in our walk with the Lord. Our children and grandchildren are well and successful. We have both been chosen to be a mother to many. I am proud to walk in your footsteps. I have so many memories of our time together. You have been the best teacher and mentor I could have ever asked for. Thank you my spiritual mother and friend. I pray we have many more years together.

Building the Walls

"Trust in the LORD with all your heart and do not lean on your own understanding. In all your ways acknowledge Him, and He will make your paths straight."
Proverbs 3:5-6, NASB

For twenty-five years I kept a wall built so I could not be vulnerable to pain. The pain was created by my fear of the death of my husband or children. I had such a fear of rejection and being left behind. These feelings made sense to me because my mother died when I was eight years old. Each time I became too happy, I would get suspicious that something bad would happen. My life was like a roller coaster ride. Each time I would choose to be happy and try to remove a brick from the wall, I would get hurt again. My wall was a prison that had became my normal way of life. The wall protected me from pain and disappointments.

As I remember, there was a year early in our marriage when I made an announcement that it was my birthday in a week. Those were the days when my children were young and my husband was always busy building his business. I wanted to please him so much that I just let my birthday go by, and did not mention it again. But inside, I felt forgotten and hurt. So I built the wall even higher. I gave up all expectations. In my thinking, pain was always connected with the possibility of death. In order to stay alive I had to keep my distance. What a sad way to live!

As soon as I started removing the bricks of my wall by trusting, an incident would usually occur for me to grab another brick and start rebuilding. I was so insecure from childhood that I carried it through to my marriage. By the time I was twenty-six, I had seven immediate members of my family were dead. I guess you can say, I made my own destiny.

Why do we allow our childhood to rule our adulthood? Why can't we be strong enough to say, "I am going to make my life better as I get older and stop the madness?"

After twenty-five years of a dysfunctional marriage, I was forced to have my wall tumble down. My husband wanted a divorce. Our marriage seemed hopeless. Yet, this became the best thing that ever happened to me. I wanted to start over with a brand new me and work on my own insecurities. It was very scary and I cried a lot. But it was the one thing I needed most. **I thank God for turning my world upside down because it forced me to change. Out of struggle comes beauty.**

Building walls does not work; you distance yourself from love and being loved. For so many years I thought I was protecting myself, when all along I was creating my own pain.

Through the years, I have realized that my life is like a flower. We start off tiny and fragile, blowing with the wind, and trying to survive. With time, our roots grow deeply and the beauty of the flower blooms into great splendor. As I pursued counseling and self-study, my confidence started to build. Over time each brick was demolished. Insecurity was replaced by self-esteem. Every time I would want to re-cement a brick back into place, I would surround myself with happy humorous people, or I would help someone else. I found that doing the things I do best like sewing, planting a flower, or writing, helped me know my own value and worth.

I now know I do have value and worth. I work everyday to remember my value. It is up to me to prove it to myself. Others can't give it to me. It is my responsibility to keep the walls down in my own life.

Each moment we stand at a fork in the road. We can choose the left fork and build walls of protection, or we can choose the right fork, bloom, and burst forth into beauty.

Chapter Three

Growing Through Pain

> *None of us knows what fiery trials we'll face; life can change in an instant.*

Give Thanks

"Music's the Medicine of the Mind"

John A. Logan

The sounds of the helicopter blades were deafening, but all I could hear in my heart and soul was myself singing the hymn by Henry Smith, "Give thanks with a grateful heart." Just hours before I had crawled away from a fiery inferno that once was our motor home. I had seen my skin melting off my arms and legs and felt excruciating pain from my back. The intense heat was literally melting me. The black billowing smoke blinded me as I looked for my husband and daughter. As I raced from the menacing flames I screamed, "Save my family! Save my family!" Now, as I lingered in a fog lying on a stretcher, all I can remember is the song that I was singing.

Earlier I was taken by ambulance to a nearby hospital to be stabilized. It was at that time I was told that my family was alive. The nurses quickly cut the clothes off my charred body and the wedding ring off my swollen finger. I could hear my adult daughter screaming, "I want my mother," over and over from the room next to mine. I kept insisting that I needed to be with her, but the three people working on me held me down. I had no idea of how extreme my injuries were. My heart was breaking with each one of her screams. They calmly kept telling me she was all right. My husband was taken by helicopter to the burn center three hours away. That was when the song started playing in my head. My family is alive, and all I wanted to do was to praise God.

"Give thanks with a grateful heart,

85

Give thanks to the Holy One
Give thanks because He's given Jesus Christ, His Son.
And now let the weak say 'I am strong,'
Let the poor say 'I am rich,'
Because of what the Lord has done for us."

As they lifted me off the helicopter, one of my good friends was there to greet me. I was trying to lift my hands as I sang. She joined in to gently help me. I kept saying, "God is good." He kept us all alive.

That song kept me going through my darkest hours. Several days passed until I awakened in my hospital room in the burn unit. Slowly, I recognized the enormity of the accident. 48% of my body was burned and my back had been broken. Our daughter was thrown through the window away from the fire but received many broken bones. My husband was lying in a coma two rooms from my own. He had fifteen fractures of his head and was 68% burned. Because of the severity of his injuries, he was given only a 9% chance of living.

I was trapped inside a severely burned body and the pain was ferocious. I had, in fact, become a prisoner within my uncontrollable shivering frame. Tears poured from my eyes, but my burned arms and hands could not reach to wipe them away.

My entire life had been full of challenges, and I knew my faith and music had always upheld me in the past. This time, I would have to trust and allow them to carry me through this healing and restoring season. I had my son bring in a CD player and my praise and worship music.   The music played all through the day and gave me encouragement.

The song, "Give Thanks," became my theme song for my bandage changes. Each day was full of extreme pain as I experienced two-hour bandage changes each morning and each night. I would ask my nurses to put my music on. As I tried to sing along, I would concentrate on each word. I found the words would give me the hope I needed to get through every painful bandage change. The nurses would sing along as they worked on me. The music helped me cope with the pain management. Whenever I thought I could not go through another minute of the procedure, I would choose to focus on my music.

The melodies played on through the challenging and happy times of my life.

Thankfully, my husband and daughter have survived. I now sing happy songs to my grandchildren and life can't get much better. We've since made it our song of hope to share our success story with burn survivors and families all over the world. I hope you too will find a song within the deep recesses of yourself to make it through life's challenging moments, knowing whatever your trial may be there is a brighter note to be sung.

First published in "Chicken Soup for the Soul – Count Your Blessings" 2009.

Hero Unaware

What does a hero look like? Could you be a hero? I feel they are walking among us every day. God might send you a hero that looks like a stranger or a friend. For my family, it was a stranger that we had never met who changed our lives forever.

On August 28, 1993, my family was in a horrible motor home accident. I was able to escape the flames through a hole in the vehicle wall. Upon impact our daughter was thrown out the front window. My husband, Rusty, was stuck in his seatbelt unable to release it. The sky was filled with black smoke as the freeway backed up for miles. Big trucks piled up trying to creep slowly by our burning motor home. People traveling north to their destinations stared in disbelief not knowing what to do. I can't imagine the horror they felt as they heard our daughter screaming for help for her family. The fiery inferno burned so quickly that by the time our daughter landed in front of the vehicle, there were no walls standing. All she could see was her father in flames trying to get his seatbelt off. She did not see me crawl out of the back of the motor home.

Out of the people who were frozen along the road that memorable day was a man named Mark. He had no idea the impact he would have on our family. He grabbed hold of his brown wool Australian hat and ran toward what was left of the burning wreckage. All he could see was a man struggling to get out. Mark pulled his hat down tightly and grabbed the charred body inside. The heat was so intense, the man's skin was melting off. Mark had to let go. He took another deep breath and once again entered into the fiery hell. This time he took hold of the man's clothing and pulled him out of the motor home. He carried the smoking image up to the road and laid him down. Mark yelled for someone to watch Rusty while he grabbed a first-aid kit out of his truck. As he walked back from his truck, he could see a black charred image walking across the freeway. My husband literally got up and walked down the road. The people who saw him must still have nightmares.

When the emergency vehicle arrived, we were all taken to the closest hospital to be stabilized. Then, we were sent to a burn center. While we were being treated, our hero Mark, was being questioned and given first aid for his burned hands.

Many months passed before we knew about our hero Mark. My husband's mother had called him several times to thank him for saving her son's life. He kept in touch with her on our progress. I don't remember when we exactly met Mark, but I know we all cried a lot and felt a brotherhood like we had never felt. We all quickly became friends and spent much time together.

Even though we live many miles apart, our hearts are connected. Because of this horrible incident, God brought something good into our family - a new brother. We seemed to know when each other had a need and would call to check in.

We will be forever thankful for this wonderful man who changed our lives that day.

Mark's famous hat still hangs in our bunkhouse. Our grandchildren know that their grandfather would not be here today if it weren't for a man they call Uncle Mark.

Have you ever wondered how you would respond if you came upon an emergency situation? Would you be frozen in place or would you be a hero like Mark? I want to believe that I would try to help. But none of us know that until the opportunity comes along.

Here are some practical ways you can be prepared to make that choice:

1.) Keep a complete first-aid kit in your car including a first aid book.
2.) Have an aluminum blanket available.
3.) Carry a couple gallons of water.
4.) Be sure to have a fire extinguisher.
5.) Learn CPR.

For myself, I know if I were prepared I would not feel as helpless.

Hope From the Ashes

I kept hearing my voice screaming, "Help me! Save my family." The deafening sounds of the roaring inferno around me drowned out the sound of my voice. In this nightmare I was seeing my own skin melting off my arms and legs as I crawled away from my family. They were trapped in the fiery inferno. I asked myself over and over, "When will I wake up from this nightmare?" After a few days I realized it was not a nightmare at all. My husband, daughter and I had really been in a horrendous motor home accident, and I was not dreaming. It was a reality. When I regained consciousness, I was informed that my daughter was in a hospital three hours away. Two doors down from my room, my husband lay unconscious in the burn unit. Thank God they were alive!

Each day I lay in a hospital bed looking out of a window watching the world go on around me. Everyone and everything seemed to be moving, except me. I was trapped inside of a severely burned body with a shattered back. The pain was like no other in this world. I now understood the term "racked with pain" as my body shook uncontrollably. Tears poured from my eyes continually, but my burned arms and hands could not reach to wipe them. I was imprisoned in a world I had never experienced.

As I watched the seasons change, I realized my life would never be the same. In the midst of the biggest challenge of my forty-seven years, I was falling into a deep pit of despair and depression. In the book, "*A Gift of Mourning Glories: Restore Your Life After Loss*" Georgia Shaffer described perfectly the darkest time in my life when she wrote, "Winter existed both on the inside and outside of me." For me, there seemed to be no sunshine. It would be that way for a very long time.

My entire life had been full of challenges. I knew my faith in Jesus had always upheld me in the past. This time I would have to trust and allow Him to carry me through this season of healing and restoring.

Life became a routine of procedures. Encased in bandages from head to toe, my first few weeks consisted of five skin grafts and one surgery to repair my broken back. The skin on my stomach had now become my donor site. Skin was harvested every three to five days. Then it was stapled in place. Because I couldn't move on those days, my muscles soon forgot how to move. Through painful rehabilitation, I had to relearn how to bend my fingers, to feed myself and take care of myself again.

By the grace of God, we all lived. My husband and I were left severely burned. There was a long journey ahead of us. Rusty lost the left side of his face, his eyesight on that side, and four fingers on his left hand. He was given only a 9% chance of living. Our daughter had many fractures including a broken back, but she was not burned.

My desires and dreams of making a difference in people's lives seemed impossible. At this time in my life I could not even take care of myself. I wanted most of all to have something good come out of this tragic incident. The one thing that helped me most during my hospital stay was when a former burn patient came into my room. He shared his story with me and showed me pictures of when he was in the hospital. Standing before me, he looked like a normal person. He did not look at all like the monster I pictured myself. He gave me a spark of hope that everything would be all right someday.

That glimmer of hope carried me through those first days and into weeks of recovery. I knew my view of life would never be the same, so I clung to my faith like never before. I listened to music that helped to lift my spirits. Each time the therapist entered the room, I repeated Phil. 4:13, NKJV, *"I can do all things through Christ who strengthens me."* And each time I repeated the verse, I felt more hopeful. That hope gave me the strength to recover more each day.

After two months of extremely painful therapy, I was able to take six steps with a nurse on each side of me. I could sit in a chair for an hour at a time. I was learning to feed myself. Emotionally, I still had a hard time and cried continually. Finally, it was time to go home. Leaving the hospital was another major adjustment.

At that time, I had a breakthrough. I realized there was an even bigger plan for me. My purpose was to touch and inspire people. Anything was possible with faith, hope, and love. That hope and love was expressed from the inside out. It took something to happen on the outside to help me realize the power of my strength within.

After a year of recovery, I was ready to start giving that hope to others. I began visiting burn survivors and their families in the hospital to encourage them. In the beginning, it was very difficult going back to the burn unit. The stark white surroundings, the ticking sounds of the machines keeping people alive, and the smells of burned skin reminded me of the most painful time in my life.

I believe Romans 8:28 is true. *"And we know that God causes all things to work together for good to those who love God, to those who are called according to His purpose."* During my quiet time in prayer I would often question, "What purpose did this accident play, and how do You want me to make a difference because of it?"

As time went by, I began to realize I had been doubly blessed. This accident had a purpose. I was a burn survivor, but also a family member of a burn survivor. I could reach many people because of my experiences. I learned when a family member was injured it was a family affair as everyone is affected. Not one of us had traveled that road and we need guidance.

The first year we had many hours of rehabilitation and much pain. The second year I began researching for doctors all over the country to put my husband's face back together. It was a miracle that we recovered so well.

As I started meeting more and more burned families, my love for them grew much stronger than humanly possible. Each time I would enter a room, I would pray for courage and God's love to show to the patient and their families.

Most severely burned people are unrecognizable in the beginning resulting in family members have a problem believing this is really their loved one. One father continually ran out of his twenty year-old daughter's room crying, "That's not my daughter!" My heart broke each time he said those words. His young daughter was a firefighter caught in a firestorm. The crew believed the fire was out, so she took off her fire gear except for her boots. It was then the flames roared up again, and she was caught in the middle. Knowing her story, I had her father look at her feet. He began weeping uncontrollably. We walked through that long journey of a difficult recovery together hand-in-hand. This beautiful girl now spends her time traveling to fire stations all through the nation speaking on fire safety to fire fighters. Something good came out of her tragedy.

For the next few years as I worked alongside patients and their families, our own recovery continued. I was shown little by little the new purpose of my life. My husband was working with a wonderful doctor in Boston to rebuild his face. We were able to support and care for each other.

I felt overcome with emotion each time a new family entered the burn unit. Even though we had traveled the same road, it was still hard for me to believe we could live through such a horrible process. My heart would go out to those that were just beginning. Being burned is the most devastating thing that can happen to a human life. Within seconds our outside appearance is stripped away. It affects all parts of our humanity - spiritual, physical, intellectual, and emotional. Each part malfunctions and needs to be rebuilt. Many patients want to die rather than face the reality of their new life. By my living example I wanted them to choose life. I did this through loving them to life!

During the second year of my recovery, I met a severely burned black woman. She had been a top surgical nurse who had now lost both of her hands and her face in a house fire. Without hands, her profession was gone. She used her experience, both as a nurse and as a trauma victim, to become a trauma counselor. This sounded simple. But she went back to school without hands and having a face at which no one wanted to look. What gives people the incredible ability to go beyond their highest expectations in spite of incredible adversity? They truly believe that nothing is impossible. When you have been through the fire and survived, you can do anything. This seems to be true even if you are left with very little physically.

The year after we were injured we learned of an organization called, "The Phoenix Society." This is an organization formed in 1977 by a burn survivor. It is based in Grand Rapids, Michigan. They help survivors from all over the world by donating educational information, giving medical advice, and supporting families. We gather together sharing a common bond every year. We meet in a different state every year for four wonderful days to hear special speakers who educate us on issues we all have. I always say, "This must be a little like heaven. No matter what the outer shell looked like, this time is filled with unconditional love."

There was usually apprehension the first time someone attended. I remembered our first conference. We entered the hotel lobby that was filled with some extremely burned people. They were laughing and talking as though they already knew each other.

We had never seen such horrible deformity, and it scared me to death. Yes, I had been working with patients in the hospital, but this was different. Most of these people looked as good as they were going to look, and yet, they seemed very happy. My heart pounded uncontrollably as we entered our room, and I did not want to come out. I told my husband, "We don't belong here." When we went to dinner that evening, we sat at a table of six. They included us in their conversation and asked us about our injuries. As we talked something magical happened. I started to realize that they experienced the same emotions as we had. Before long, I no longer noticed their scars. We had all experienced the stares and comments of the people on the outside. For four special days a year, we had each other and were totally accepted.

Over the past years I have worked with forty to fifty families. I have spoken at many burn retreats and have been very involved with the World Burn Congress. Each Congress has been special as I watch many of these same families get involved to help themselves transcend beyond their circumstances. (That is a term we use, meaning that we are better after the incident than we were before).

Each year I meet some new special people that felt as I did in the beginning. They felt as if they were dead when they arrived. But by the end of the congress, they were reborn. Many old acquaintances are renewed. It was hard for me to explain the joy and pride I felt to see young people that I watched struggle for their lives in the beginning, bloom into strong, beautiful people. I listened to their accomplishments, and no matter what, they overcame their obstacles. The tears rolled down my cheeks with pride that they chose to take an insurmountable situation and turned it into something good. They wear their scars as a badge of courage.

Today my life is fuller than I could ever imagine. My husband, daughter and I are completely healed. I am grateful for every part of the changes it took to make me the woman I am. Without this experience I wouldn't have met some of the greatest and bravest over-comers on this earth.

My purpose is to give inspiration not only to people disabled by accidents and struggling to lead some kind of a normal life, but to all of us that have suffered setbacks in our lives. We feel that fate has treated us unfairly but still believe that we can make something of our lives if we only knew how. I did learn how. Now I am grateful I can share it with others

I have run across some incredible people who have taught me what I hadn't truly known before - generosity, humility, and concern for others. I pray for God's love to shine through me so others will be inspired and choose life!

First published in "Comfort for the Grieving Heart" 2002.

God Supplies Angels

"Therefore my heart is glad and my glory rejoices;
my flesh will also rest in hope."
Psalm 16:9, NKJV

I lay flat on my back staring at the ceiling. It was late at night, and I could see shadows from the nurses' station shining through the glass door into my room. I could hear the beeping of the machines around me. Each time I inhaled, I breathed the horrible smell of the yellow *Xeroform* bandages that covered my raw, burned skin. I had been in a major motor home fire, and I was 48% burned. My back was shattered and broken. Within seconds, my life had been dismantled. Just two doors away from me in the burn unit, my husband lay in a coma. He had been given only a 9% chance of living. I missed him so much and did not want to live without him.

Each night was like the night before. I lay there waiting for the night nurse to come and hurt me with the two-hour bandage change. My depression and anxiety continued to grow. Nighttime seemed the worst time. I could not sleep. My thoughts were filled with doubt and little hope.

I remembered one night vividly. My finger did a yo-yo motion with the call button. I did not want to bother the nurses, but I did need to talk to someone. The burn unit is busy, and one of the hardest places in the hospital to work. However, my emotional pain won the battle and I rang. One of the night nurses, Joan, entered my room. She was a tall, thin woman in her fifties who usually worked days. I was so glad to see her. She always called me her prize patient. She tried to listen to me when she had time.

"What's going on with you tonight?" she asked. "Are you in pain? Why aren't you asleep?"

"Asleep" was a post-traumatic trigger word for me. I was asleep when the accident happened, so I rarely slept now. Somehow in my emotional state, I thought the accident would not have occurred if I had been awake. In my drug-induced stupor I felt I needed to be on night duty, so I could be in control. When a person is burned, all four parts that make up our humanity are affected: emotional, spiritual, physical, and intellectual. Each is damaged and needs to be healed. My pain was continual. So was my fear of going to sleep. No matter what drugs they gave me, it was impossible to shake.

As Joan stood in front of me, I noticed the pretty, shiny gold earrings she was wearing. I started to share with her some of my fears I felt that I now looked like a monster.

"Will anyone accept me the way I look now?"

Joan pulled a chair beside me and listened. "Will I ever be normal again, or pretty, or able to walk?" I sobbed. "Will this pain ever go away? Will I be able to feed myself and put on pretty earrings again?"

Abruptly, Joan stopped me. "Have you looked at your face yet?" she asked. "No, I am afraid to," I cried. She immediately got up and left the room. I feared what was going to happen next.

As Joan reentered the room, she had a mirror in her hand. "No!" I shouted. "I am afraid to look!" I had seen my arms and legs during the bandage change and I knew I looked like a freak.

She came closer to me and started to brush my hair quietly saying, "You are pretty. Your face is all right. It is rosy with first-degree burns, but that will go away." Then she took her earrings off and clipped them to my ears. My tears gushed uncontrollably as I found the courage to look in the mirror.

For five weeks I had wondered what my face looked like. Now I knew. Thanks to a nurse named Joan who took the time to listen and help me through this important transition, I now had hope. All would be well someday.

Susan adds, "It took nearly a decade and numerous plastic surgeries before the love of my life was back to normal. Rusty is now able to work as he did before the accident. We are thankful for each day we have together."

First published in "Chicken Soup for the Nurse's Soul – Second Dose" 2007
Reprinted in the Phoenix Society "Burn Support News" 2007.

Sisters In All Seasons

"Do to others whatever you would like them to do to you. This is the essence of all that is taught in the law and the prophets"
Matt. 7:12, NLT

Lying in my hospital bed, I cried. As I waited for my friends to arrive to spend their Thursday night with me, I remembered all of the times we had shared over the past twenty-five years. Even though our family had moved ten years prior, our sisterhood stayed faithful.

A horrendous accident had turned my life upside down. My husband, Rusty, adult daughter Nikki, and I had been in a motor home accident. We were all badly injured and severely burned. Since that fateful night, my friends had been driving four hours round trip every Thursday after work to be with me.

As I waited for them to arrive, my thoughts drifted back to our early twenties when we first met in Woman's Bible Study Fellowship. We were all young wives and mothers trying to grow in our faith. Through time, our relationships grew too. We experienced many life difficulties together, problems with our children, separation from our husbands, drug addiction, failing parents, and many other issues.

My friends became family to me. We were always there for each other. Even though there had been separation by distance, we still planned special times together each year. We made a pact with ourselves to never lose touch – even if we only made a phone call each week. We had too much history together, and that could never be taken from us and never replaced.

During different seasons of our lives, I felt the friendships were one-sided. Yet in difficult times, we were there for each other. Many times I would almost give up on the friendships. I was always the initiator. As time went by without contact from one of them, I would always give in and call. I remember at one time saying, "I will not call her again," as I marked the date on the calendar to remind myself. I ended up calling because I missed her.

As I recall that memory, I think how the Lord must feel when He doesn't hear from us. Isn't it wonderful that He doesn't give up on us either? Some way or the other, He'll get our attention. I guess you can say He doesn't wait to call.

During this most challenging time in my life, I knew I could trust and depend on my sisters in the Lord. Right after the accident, there was nothing anyone could do but wait and pray. My husband and I were both on a live-or-die list. He stayed on the list for the first two months. I was taken off after a week. From that point my friends took a silent oath that they would not stop coming to be with me until they knew I would be all right.

I knew it was hard on them. They sacrificed to travel so far. Just entering my room was difficult. Some people would get sick to their stomachs; others actually fainted. But these dear friends kept coming back each week to encourage me.

Just to enter my room you had to wear gown, gloves, and a mask to prevent infection. The smell of burned skin and the medications was nauseating. The room was kept hot with no fresh air to breath. I looked like a monster all wrapped with white gauze and weeping fluids coming through. I was unable to do a single task for myself. Because my back was broken, I had to lie totally flat and not move, but I could smile. They made sure I did!

There were questions about how much movement I would have and if I would ever walk again. None of us had even known a burned person before so there were many questions about how I would end up looking. My friends tried to find a book to help them understand burns so they could help me. No books were easily available at that time.

I remember the first time my friends took me downstairs in a wheelchair to a burn support group meeting. All four of us were scared to death of what we would see and hear. They asked a lot of questions. All I could do was cry. We were living in a world none of us understood.

Once I was released from the hospital after two long months, those same friends continued to visit each Thursday for six months. They were there for me when I learned to take my first steps of recovery. They were my prayer warriors, my comforters, and my counselors. I depended on them sharing each aching moment of pain and concern with them.

I remember the night before I was to see my husband for the first time since the accident. I had refused to see him until I knew he was going to live. I did not want to have my last memory of Rusty being hooked to tubes and badly burned. We had been together since I was fifteen, and I wanted to remember the good times. It had been ten weeks since the incident and I was much stronger. I could finally feed myself, and take a few steps. Rusty had awakened out of his coma, and I was told that he would live.

Our son had gone to the hospital to take Polaroid pictures of him to show me when my friends arrived. Each one sat beside me in a circle as we began to pass the pictures. I can't express the fear I felt. The room was silent except for sobbing.

It was a sad season in all of our lives, made better because we shared it together. There were many people who took part in our full recovery. Our neighborhood rallied around to help in many ways. My local Bible study girls took turns feeding, walking, rubbing, and exercising me. They all walked the journey with us and had a part in seeing a success story as our happy ending came true.

The Lord said, *"And we know that in all things God works for the good of those who love him, who have been called according to his purpose."* Romans 8:28, NIV. The sacrifice of many friends and the power of prayer healed my family.

First published in "Divine Stories of the Yahweh Sisterhood" 2006.

God's Answer to Prayer

"I've been driven many times to my knees by the
overwhelming conviction that I had nowhere
else to go. My own wisdom, and that of all about
me, seemed insufficient for the day."

Abraham Lincoln

Within a matter of minutes, our lives were transferred from happy and healthy, to sad and hopeless. My husband and I barely survived a horrendous motor home accident that would change our lives forever. During my two-month stay in the burn ward, I had many skin grafts and a surgery to fuse my back. I would lie in the hospital, wondering how I was ever going to be able to care for myself again, let alone care for him. I prayed for God to send someone to help me when I was released.

God sent my niece, Vikki, who was a home-health aid, to be with me twenty-four hours a day for the next five months. My husband, Rusty, was still recovering in the hospital. When she first came to live with me, we were not close. Because of her expertise in nursing and my need for her help, our relationship became an everlasting bond.

In the beginning, I had to re-learn to do the simplest of human chores, like walking and eating. I had many other caregivers in and out of our home. Each morning, a nurse came to change my bandages. It took two hours. In the afternoon a physical therapist arrived. There were usually five or six people coming and going each day. There was heaps of laundry to do each day and quite often the neighbors provided good meals. I had many appointments to make and keep. I also had a lot of therapy and exercises to do on my own.

In the midst of it all, Vikki was my protector, mentor, and helper. Weekly visits to both the burn doctor and back doctor usually took two to three hours because of full doctors' offices. Vikki taught me how to solve this problem. As if I didn't look pathetic enough already, she put me in the wheelchair, puffed a little powder on my face and told me to drool! It seemed to work because they started taking me immediately. Through it all, we laughed a lot. Vikki kept everything going. Thank God!

Every fear I had in my life reoccurred with the trauma of this accident. Vikki not only had to deal with my physical injuries, but also my psychological needs. I was such a mess. She taught me to be strong and wouldn't allow others to baby me. She taught me to do things for myself again. Many times she had to say to me, "JUST GET OVER IT." I couldn't believe her persistence and perseverance. She taught me well that love must be tough. I remember not liking her many times because she made me do things that hurt. At times other family members seemed jealous of our relationship. We shared the pain, tears, and sense of humor that it took for me to recover. I trusted the Lord to send me the right person to help me through this experience. And He definitely did.

While all of this was going on at home, my husband was still in the hospital. It took two months for him to wake up from the coma, and many more months of recovery before he could come home too. He had fifteen fractures of his head, lost four fingers of his left hand, his left eye and the left side of his face was severely burned. He was declared legally blind. I knew how hard and painful it was learning to take care of myself. I knew he would have to go through the same process and longed for the day I could help him.

It took nine months for me to be able to be his caregiver. Thanks to my niece, I was finally able to take care of myself. In time, we no longer needed a caregiver living with us. At first I was very frightened to be on our own. Vikki had taught me how to help him by making him realize that he was a survivor, not a victim. It was so difficult to watch him struggle learning to dress himself and putting on his shoes with one hand. At times, I felt more like his mother than his wife, and had little patience. Every movement seemed to be in slow motion. When I felt like giving up, I would tap into all the kindness but firmness my Vikki had taught me. He had to learn to do things for himself again. Many times I had to say, "JUST GET OVER IT." I couldn't believe MY persistence and perseverance.

By the grace of God, we made it through those challenging eight years of healing and we are closer than ever before. We are proud to tell our success story.

My husband often shares how he, too, had laid in the hospital praying that God would send the right person to help him. Then he kisses my cheek and says, "He did. He sent me you!"

First published in "Chicken Soup for the Caregiver's Soul" 2004.

108

Reap What We Sow

"Remember this - a farmer who plants just a few seeds will get a small crop. But the one who plants generously will get a generous crop"
2 Cor. 9:6, Living.

"I won't leave," Frank said as he stood in front of the nurse's station. He was overtaken by the smell of burned skin and the sounds of the life saving monitors in the stark surroundings. The man he had known as his role model since he was fifteen had been badly injured and severely burned. The nurses had just told him, "Only family members allowed." He officially was not family and did not share the same last name. The nurses did not understand that this young man was as much a son to us as our own.

In the early years our family was filled with laughter and tears. My husband and I had two busy children of our own. More arrived when they needed places to stay. They came and went as they needed. We never adopted any of the children. We just had an open door policy. I loved children so my nurturing heart considered each one my own. My husband loved work and provided well for all of us.

As everyone grew into adults and found their own way in life, most kept in touch with us. I was amazed how they needed me when they were young, but grew very close to my husband as adults. They always went to him for advice in business and finances as he was always there to help them.

Frank was one of the boys who lived in our home off and on since the age of fifteen. He had stayed very close to us as an adult. Frank was in his late twenties when we were in a horrendous accident.

Finally, Frank was cleared to go into my husband's hospital room. He stood by his bed watching the man he loved wrapped in white bandages from head to toe. The ventilator was breathing for him, and the sounds of the monitors were the only indicators of life. It was at that moment that Frank had decided to stand and fight this fight for life with the man he knew as "Dad."

Frank's routine was to go to work during the day and spend the night sitting next to his Dad. He watched as the nurses changed the bandages and the procedures that were required to prevent infection. He asked questions constantly during the cycle of ups and downs for the first two months his Dad lay in a coma.

We all sighed with relief when Rusty was moved out of the burn unit into the rehabilitation unit. Now it was time for him to learn to feed himself, learn to walk and talk all over again. Frank increased his hours at the hospital to help with this long painful process. He became very protective of his Dad and learned everything he could to help Rusty when the nurses were sometimes not available. This adopted son would make sure he was there each time the therapist exercised Rusty so he could learn to do the stretching in preparation for Rusty to walk.

Walking was complicated as Rusty's injuries consisted of 68% burn with loss of the left side of his face and eye. He was now legally blind. He also had four of his left fingers amputated. There was much work and reconstruction left to do when he was released from the hospital four months after he entered.

When we learned the date of release, there was not an option in Frank's mind what he needed to do. All he thought about when he was at work was his Dad and the care he was receiving. He ran on adrenaline and seemed obsessed with Rusty's care. Rusty was reluctant when it came time to come home. "Who was going to help me?" he asked. Frank knew the procedures, so he gave up his day job and became Rusty's full-time caregiver. Rusty was relieved and trusted him feeling very comfortable with the arrangement.

I still needed full time care. My caregiver was also one of the children who came in and out of our home. She was my niece and worked as a home health aid. She also gave up her job to move in and help me recuperate.

Many of our other children were in and out of our home. We encouraged them to go on with their own lives as much as possible. Life as we knew it had changed, but we were all still together.

Rusty had a long way to go. Each day the routine seemed the same. Frank took control and was firm but loving with his demands. Rusty needed to learn to do things for himself again. It seems when a person is in the hospital for a long period of time, they fall into the victim role instead of the survivor mode. The roles were reversed. Now Frank was the son helping his father get better, and that was difficult at times. I think role reversal is a big obstacle when a family member becomes the caregiver. It is hard to move out of the parent-child relationship.

As Rusty started to want to take control of his own life, Frank felt apprehensive even though we had all prayed for this. It was much like knowing when to let our children go even if it meant letting them stumble and fall. One of the not-so-fond memories was when Rusty insisted on driving his truck again. Frank drove him to a large parking lot and had Rusty get into the driver's seat. Frank sat in the passenger seat praying.

Frank went back to work after five months helping his Dad learn not only to be a survivor but a thriver. He still came by daily to check his progress. If you would ask Frank today if he would do it all again, he wouldn't hesitate a moment in saying, "It was a terrible time in life, but I learned perseverance, patience, and unconditional love through it all. It was my time to give back. The power of prayer was proven over and over again."

"Reap what we sow" is exactly what God was showing us through this season in our lives. We have wonderful children, our own, plus others that had a time in their lives when they needed someone to love them. They were all there for us when we were in need. We all learned so many lessons during that time in our lives. Most of all, life can change in a moment. Love and support each other while we can.

My Experience as a Burn Survivor

Before I was burned, I felt I had experienced some of the hardest challenges of my life. I had gone through the loss of my parents and siblings at an early age, marriage difficulties, and drug addiction with my son. When I was burned in a motor home accident in August, 1993, little did I know that the recovery would be the biggest challenge of my life! Since my husband and I were so badly burned, I jumped feet first into learning as much as I could about what lay ahead of us in our new life. I researched every area of need that we had.

I was genuinely surprised at the many "issues" we burn survivors have to face and overcome. The bodily injury is just the tip of the iceberg. I came to realize burn survivors have a very unique recovery process unlike any other type of injury. I started volunteering at University of California at Davis and Shriner's Hospitals to help meet the needs of other burn survivors. I felt my experience in counseling before I was burned was invaluable. My ambition and commitment was to help other survivors travel through this extremely painful time in their lives. It was exceptional to experience playing the dual role of burn survivor and family member. I felt it a duty to help both categories. The need was great.

I was honored to be able to attend the American Burn Association (ABA). It was both awakening and educational. I was awed by the progress in new advancements made since my own burn injury. The commitment of the professionals was outstanding. Some of the doctors who spoke we were privileged to have cared for us during our hospital stay. Now I was able to know them as friends and colleagues. It was an advantage to my own psychological healing. I have developed great admiration for those who work in this most difficult field.

During ABA, I sat and listened to classes where research papers were presented from the professional and clinical standpoint. However, I wanted to give them the viewpoint of a survivor who lived through the experience. When I spoke I focused the majority of my time on the psychosocial issues I faced such as PTSD (Post Traumatic Stress Disorder), pain management, discharge anxiety, and integration into society. I hoped that hearing my opinions enlightened health care workers to better care for their patients.

When I awakened in the hospital, I realized the nightmare I was experiencing was really true. I experienced the devastation of my injuries and inability to do anything about it. I had no control over my situation including the fact that my daughter was hurt in a hospital two hours away and my husband was dying two rooms down from my own. Life as I knew it was over. While I watched the bandage changes every day and saw my arms and legs skinned, I thought I must look like a monster. The pain was so extreme that concentration on anything, TV, visitors, music, or instructions from nurses and therapists, was hard to absorb. The feelings of hopelessness were unbelievable. Not being able to control anything in my life took me back to total infancy. These experiences made it hard for me to believe that anyone severely burned could escape Post Traumatic Stress Disorder (PTSD). I suffered greatly from PTSD. At times, even today, memories trigger difficult feelings.

No matter how much pain medication was given, the horror never went away. The drugs could take the edge off my pain, but the reality still remained. Music was my saving grace. I would concentrate on the words making the bandage changes somewhat bearable. But anxiety was always present with me. Anticipation of the bandage changes twice a day would cause constant fear. Perhaps, if I had known approximate times of the procedures, my fear would have lessened. I knew this process of removing dead skin was necessary, but it was the most unbearable part of the injury. At times today when I am with patients I wonder, "How did we ever live through this ordeal?" What a hard job for the staff to cause such pain to make me well. I wanted them to know no matter how much pain we felt, even if a person was on a respirator, we remembered words and the attitude with which they treated us. We wore our emotions on our sleeves. It was a very sad time in our lives. I wanted to share that no matter how badly we looked, we were still there inside. After I spent time in the hospital working along with nurses and therapists, we learned whom we could trust.

When it was time to be discharged, the anxiety level became even higher. We didn't know who would care for us at home. Life at home would not be the same we knew. I grew anxious lying in the hospital room thinking about the way we looked, now knowing the pictures on the wall at home would be of someone who looked so differently. We were anxious to see our friends, family, and pets, but soon realizing they were just as afraid to see us, as we were to see them. Our smell was different, as well as our looks, so animals tended to stay away for a while. Even small children approached us with uncertainty. All the daily tasks, such as walking, feeding, brushing our own teeth, getting a drink of water, all took energy. So I wondered how I would ever take care of myself again. I was accepted by those in the burn unit, but feared, "How would I be accepted outside?" These were just a few of the thoughts running through my head as I approached discharge.

Integrating into society was another challenge. After the physical healing was coming along, we still had the emotional healing to deal with. We knew that our burn scars were forever. So we needed to mourn the loss of our old self, begin to accept our lives, and to be grateful for what we had left. Some of our hopes and dreams, goals and desires had been rearranged. It was a time to work and to learn how to accept ourselves. I found that if a survivor had not experienced that process before the injury, it was doubly difficult afterwards. Many had chosen to hide their scars by wearing clothes that would keep them hidden. Some chose only to go out at night so people wouldn't stare. Others became angry and embittered by what has happened to them. They needed to know that their looks might not keep people away, but their actions and attitude would.

An important part of the physical and emotional healing of a burn survivor is being accepted as part of the burn team on the burn unit. The old saying, "It takes one to know one," is certainly true in this situation. Having a mentor who has experienced some of the same emotions is invaluable. My desire was to see the Phoenix Society train burn volunteers to take on this important role. I knew from my own experiences that the doctors and nurses do not have the time to explain everything to families at the beginning of the injury. I learned that research showed that families were the most important support for the patient. If a volunteer could be with them from the beginning, to explain and support them through this shocking and devastating time, the family would be able to support their loved one in a much healthier way. It took building a relationship with the family and the survivor when the time was right to make this nightmare bearable. Not everyone had a supporting family at home, yet all could learn how to nurture the burn survivor through our example.

I look back on the entire incident with an enlightened outlook and renewed hope. We are all so very special in this life. I say this from my own experience that brought this simple fact into clear and perfect focus for me.

Victors Not Victims

Years ago, my life was changed in an instant with one horrendous accident. My family was in a near-fatal motor home accident, and we were severely burned. I went from a happy, secure, healthy person to a helpless, insecure victim. I was totally helpless. It soon turned into hopelessness. I knew our lives would never be the same again.

When the September 11th tragedy occurred, I was once again reminded how fast circumstances can change our lives. Just as my life had changed, in a matter of moments our country's freedom had been threatened. Millions of lives have been affected. The horror and fear of the unknown has touched each one of us. The loss of so many loved ones has left us all stunned and shocked. It could have happened to anyone of us. Since I experienced a life-changing incident myself, I KNOW how true that statement is. We have all been shaken by this horrible act of terrorism. While watching the grief of so many during this overwhelming time of loss, I remembered all of the questions I asked myself as I laid in my hospital bed. The shock and unbearable pain I experienced was unbelievable. I wondered how this could have happened? How and what could I do to change it or make it better? Whose fault was it? The undeniable fear of the unknown fell upon our country. What would happen to our country and how would this event change all of our lives?

Just like in my own life, it has brought people back together in unity. Life, as we knew it, has been changed forever. This event has taken our eyes and thoughts off ourselves and put them back on the

Lord. Our country has once again looked up to our Lord for unity, hope, and strength. Our God is crying right along with us. This sadness that we all feel, He feels too. I was sorry that it took something so horrendous to shake our country's freedom costing so many lives. Just as I had to experience painful rehabilitation to be restored, day-by-day and month-by-month, God will carry us through this tragedy by His guidance and grace.

During my time of restoration I claimed the Bible verse Phil. 4:13, NKJV, *"I can do all things through Christ who strengthens me."* Our family had fallen into a life of complacency. We had taken the simple things in life for granted. Today, we are able to do all things once again as we have been restored. As individuals, we are better than we were before if we always remember, "God is in Control." We as a country will get through this time, and we will overcome. We have enjoyed this great freedom for many decades. God has blessed America. Now let's bless Him by renewing our faith in Him.

Our great America started with "In God We Trust." Our lives depend on all of us standing in unity, believing and trusting the One who created the greatest free country in the world. "GOD KEEP BLESSING AMERICA."

Hurt But Not Destroyed

August 28, 1993 was my "September 11th." That particular day started like any other day. By the end of the day, I was lying in a hospital bed wondering if my life was over. My family and I were in a horrendous motor home accident. The magnitude of the event was unbelievable. We were left severely burned, broken, stunned and in shock.

Even though there were eight years between our accident and September. 11, I realized the process of emotional recovery was the same. I experienced the five steps of grief: shock, denial, anger, acceptance, and forgiveness.

When you have been a victim of a trauma, whether it is small or large, you still have the same journey to travel. We were in a life-and-death situation. My husband was severely burned with only a 9% chance of survival. Our daughter was badly injured. She was taken to a hospital three hours away from the burn hospital where my husband and I were. I broke my back and was burned over 48% of my body. Our lives were changed in a matter of moments.

As I watched the series of events unfold before me on September 11th, my emotions and prayers went to the thousands of victims who were affected that day. First, those who were trapped in the fiery inferno captured my prayers. I remembered the extreme heat in our accident that felt like hell to me. I watched my skin melt as I crawled away. Second, the firefighters who became my heroes since our incident needed my prayers. Many became my personal friends in the years that passed. We were actively involved in burn support where we were privileged to meet many incredible heroes.

My thoughts and feelings compelled me to do something to help. As I listened to reports of burn survivors, my thoughts went back to the pain and the long process of recovery. Life as we had known it disappeared in a matter of seconds. One moment we were able to take care of ourselves, and the next moment we had no control at all. The trauma was so great we felt this must be happening to someone else.

As I watched the family members search for their loved ones and listened to their personal stories, I remembered how many lives were affected by any trauma. With only our family involved, we used to say that we could fill up a large hotel with the many people who were touched by our family's incident. I imagined the number touched by this disaster was in the millions from that fateful day of September 11th.

As the week went on my shock turned to obsession. I didn't want to miss a piece of news. The more I heard, the sadder I became. I suffered greatly from depression after my own accident, and I was recognizing those same symptoms happening again. I knew I was feeling the pain right along with those immediately involved in the trauma of September 11th. I understood what they were experiencing and prayed for everyone night and day.

The only way I could get through my own personal pain was to listen to Praise and Worship music during the day. In the night hours I listened to the Bible on tape. It reminded me that God who was in control loved me very much. Most of all, I was reminded that He is always there for me. Even though my husband of twenty-eight years was near death and my daughter was so far away in another hospital, I knew God allowed what seemed like a little U-turn in my life. I found that my own recovery improved as I started working and helping others through this new unplanned life. The Lord encouraged me to write my memories of our incident and to share my writings with others through books and speaking engagements.

None of us knows why these things happen to us, for life will always be uncertain. I know truly through my own experiences how difficult and long the process is. So many people told me, "Time heals." I really hated hearing that, but the truth is, it can. Time will never take away the pain and memories, but it will guide us to the choices God has for us. For me, the more involved I became in the new world of burns and helping others, the faster the time sped by. My own healing was taking place. God worked through me to touch other lives through this tragedy.

It has been a very long journey and I am happy to say that God is so faithful. He answered all of our prayers and has restored our family again. My husband is legally blind and has lost many body parts, but he is well and happy. Our daughter is back at 100%. I am able to walk. We wear our burn scars as our badges of courage. Without our faith in God, I don't believe we would ever have made it through this fiery trial.

Chapter Four

Growing Beyond the Circumstances

> *Unfortunately, scars are forever, but we all have a choice on how we carry them. We can go into hiding and covering up, or we can accept them and grow.*

Moving Out of Hiding into Freedom

Have you ever sat and looked at your scars and said phrases similar to these? "I HATE my scars." "I HATE the pain," and "I HATE people staring at me!" Many days I remember just saying, "Okay! I'm tired of being burned. I just want it to go away, NOW."

Unfortunately, scars are forever, but we all have a choice on how we carry them. We can go into hiding and covering up or we can accept them and grow. I know it is not that easy because I went through the journey myself.

I have known many adults burned as children. I find many carry much shame. Children can be cruel and say mean things that hurt to the core. When you are young, you try to hide so no one will see that you are different.

A friend of mine hid his scars for some forty years. He was burned at age four. Many children made fun of him. His scars formed his view of life making his life very painful. After coming to WBC (World Burn Conference) last year, his life as a burn survivor has changed. As he says in his own words, "I was a closet burn victim. After hearing and seeing others that were free to be themselves without shame or condemnation, I myself felt free." He mentally understands the word "freedom" and now he has to incorporate it into his heart.

As I have worked alongside of others that have been burned, I see so many ways of coping with the changes that come with the injuries. My husband was also burned in our accident. He has a facial disfigurement and lost four fingers on his left hand. After watching his adjustment, I started realizing that those who have an outward burn sometime accept it better than those of us who can hide our injuries.

We have a choice. They do not.

I was forty-seven years old when I was burned. I could hide my arms and legs. I went through many stages of recovery. These were a few:

* Pain and depression (not wanting to live)

* Adjustment to wearing the burn garments for two years (fear of pain)

* Feelings of gratefulness because my garments covered my scars (hiding)

* Reality of uncovering scars when my garments came off (fear of acceptance)

* Scars - whether to uncover and be proud of what I had lived through, or cover with shame (acceptance)

I realized that even though I knew myself I had scars, many others did not even notice. Many times our own perception we have inside of ourselves is more extreme than what others can see with their eyes.

Do any of these stages sound familiar to any of you? It is a long road to freedom, and I am sure many of us travel it in different ways. We can't change what has happened to us, but we can change what we do with it. CHOICE is my key word. We all have a choice each morning how we are going to go through the day. My body might be burned, but I am left with a healthy mind and the experience to help others travel the same road I have been on.

My freedom came when I started helping others travel their long road to their new life.

Published in the Phoenix Society "Burn Support News" 2007.

The Three Transformations of Rusty

How would you like to be married to someone who has changed into three different people? This is a story about just that! I have been married to the same man for four decades. But as I reflect back, I can see three major transformations.

The first was after twenty-five turbulent years of marriage. We had raised our children, built a successful business, experienced unfaithfulness, been separated several times, and went through drug addiction with our son. My life had definitely been filled with opportunity to rely on my faith and to let God be in control. After an eight-month separation with the divorce papers ready to sign, my prayers were finally answered when my husband accepted the Lord. Before his conversion Rusty had been buried in his work and we barely communicated. He was always a good provider, but the main ingredient we were missing in our marriage was the Lord.

Now he was willing to work on our marriage through Christian counseling. He desired only to make Christ the center of our relationship. All my prayers had been answered. We had a second wedding ceremony in our church. I was in my beautiful white gown, we both had new rings on our fingers, and our daughter sang, "Let's Begin Again."

Begin again is exactly what we did. My handsome man looked the same, but was completely changed. He semi-retired and moved our business home. For two years and five months, it felt like we now were living the life I had only dreamed.

Then our lives were completely turned upside-down once again.

We left our home on a beautiful day and were traveling in our motor home with our adult daughter, Nikki, towards Oregon. Rusty and Nikki were sitting up front while I was asleep in the back. Unfortunately, my husband did not see the ditch covered in tall grass as he pulled over to stop along the shoulder of the freeway. In front of the ditch was a concrete culvert. We hit it going forty-five miles per hour. Our home on wheels crashed bursting into flames.

Once again I was screaming for God to help and save us. I felt I was in a nightmare and I could not wake myself up. I looked for a way to escape and screamed loudly for my family. The flames were separating us, and I could not see them. I yelled for God to get us out as I spotted a hole in the sidewall. I could not stand up because of the stabbing pain in my back so I crawled towards it. As I dropped outside the motor home, I immediately tried to crawl away from the flames. I could see the liquid rolling off my arms and legs, but all I could think about was that I was leaving my family in that fiery inferno. I yelled to God, "Please take us all or leave us all." I did not want to live without them.

I remember awakening days later and being told the extent of the accident. My family was alive, but we were all badly injured. Our daughter, Nikki, was thrown out on impact. Although she escaped the fire, her back was broken. I was 48% burned and also had a broken back. Rusty had fifteen fractures of his head. He was 68% burned and the left side of his face was gone. He had only a 9% chance of living. All I could do was pray God's will for his life.

I had just become used to this wonderful man that God had totally transformed. It was a long hard comeback we both had to travel. Months later we were both out of the hospital, but it took over a year to be able take care of ourselves alone. Now we had to get used to our new life as burn survivors. This hard journey has taught us many lessons.

In a matter of moments our external appearance had totally changed from two attractive people full of life, to a mass of melted skin and missing body parts. My husband was now legally blind as he was missing the left side of his face including his eye. Four of his fingers had to be removed. We had a lot of adjustments to make. Through the power of God and many caring family and friends, we made it through the long, hard journey. It took us five years for Rusty to heal and for both of us to regain some sense of normality to our lives. The first transformation was the inside. The second was one you could see in a mirror.

The third transformation made him into the man he is today. I am so proud of who Rusty has become through this journey. Since we were burned, our lives have blossomed more than I could have imagined. My husband did not just survive this challenging experience, he let God remake him into one of the most humble, loving, and caring people I know. It was incredibly difficult watching people stare at us while we were in our burn garments and throughout the surgeries that followed. I do not recall my husband ever becoming angry, irritable or resentful.

None of us knows what our lives will be like in the future. God does have a plan for each and every one of us. My first twenty-five years of marriage were years of preparation. It has not been an easy life, but it has been a life full of opportunities to show God's glory. I am grateful that I learned early to rely on God's unconditional love.

We now work with others who have to walk this long journey. We know first-hand that beauty is only skin deep wearing our burn scars as a badge of courage.

Rusty is a quiet man who walks proudly. He has traveled down a road of success on the inside and out. He has proven that money cannot buy his outside appearance or health.

"And we know that God causes all things to work together for good to those who love God, to those who are called according to His purpose." Rom. 8:28, NASB.

A Day in New York

Murder, rape, purse snatching, and one crime after another in a city that never sleeps was what I watched on NYPD week after week from the safety of my home in California. When my husband would have business meetings in New York, I was always leery about venturing out on my own without him to protect me. I got very brave or very bored one time we were visiting. Rusty had meetings all day in an office a couple of blocks from 5th Avenue and 32nd Street. With my cell phone and city map in hand, I braved the elements of New York City.

I love the electronic stores that bargain. I wanted to purchase a new little camera that I could put into my tightly secure shoulder bag. At my first stop, the owner was determined to sell me the camera, plus a few other items.

After a successful purchase, I entered the streets again only to realize that I was walking against the traffic of very fast moving people. Quickly, I moved to the right side and observed most were wearing black with their cell phones pasted to their ears. I too, was wearing black and knew I needed to talk on my cell phone. So I called my daughter in California. Now I fit in perfectly, that is until the phone started to beep to tell me low battery. WHOOPS!

My second stop was the Barnes and Noble bookstore on 5th Avenue. I have had quite a few stories published in the book series *"Chicken Soup,"* and I wanted to see if these books were on their shelves. As I entered the huge store, I asked a clerk if she could show me where the inspirational books would be. I became so excited at the thought that my name would be in this store; I found it hard to contain myself. Actually, I did not do it very well. I picked up the first book I was in, went to the content page, found my name and started to shout to the sweet clerk, "This is me! Susan Lugli. That's my name!" I didn't stop there. I went on to two other books with my name. The clerk became just as excited and started to share this news with others around her. She said, " I hope I am not busy today so I can read your stories." I felt very proud of myself as I entered back to the streets of New York.

Third stop was to see the Christmas decorations at Saks Fifth Avenue. As I entered the store, I asked a clerk if it would be all right if I took some pictures of the beautiful decorations. She announced, "I have worked here for thirty years and no one has ever asked to take pictures. They just do it! Thank you for asking." I didn't want them to think I was casing the joint or something. As I was snapping pictures with my new camera, a lady from behind the makeup counter confronted me, "Can I do your makeup for you today?" She asked politely. I said, "Thank you very much, but I do not need a thing today. No matter what you try to sell me I will not buy it." She did not care! Can you imagine she just wanted to do my face? I was thrilled! We talked for an hour while she made me look as beautiful as I felt. As I left the store I kept thinking, "What a great day so far!"

I knew it was after lunchtime because my stomach was telling me, "Feed me!" I spotted a Subway and ordered my lunch. After seeing only one chair available, I asked a gentleman if I could sit with him. We had a good talk, and he pointed me in the direction of Radio City Music Hall. As I got closer, I could see the line forming for the matinee. The one and only thing I always loved about New York were the plays. But this time we had no plans to go.

I stood in front of the billboard to see what was playing. It read, "*The Radio City Christmas Spectacular with the Rockettes.*" Oh my gosh! All I could think of was I wished I could go. As the line was going in a woman approached me and asked, "Have you seen this before?" I quickly answered, "No." "Would you like to?" she continued. "Oh yes, but I think it is too late to get a ticket," I replied. She then told me that she went every year and that it is wonderful to see. But today she had a ticket she would not need so she would like to give it to me. At that point I knew I was having a very blessed day. I offered to pay her for the ticket but she said, "I want to bless you." WOW, I couldn't believe it! We gave each other a hug. I followed the people into the hall and found my seat next to an elderly couple. Of course, I had to express my excitement to them. They had seen this spectacular many times, but I felt as if I were ten years old with the treat of my life.

The Rockettes were faultless and beautiful, complete with singers, ice skaters, and children dancing. I found myself many times grabbing the man's arm next to me saying, "Isn't this great!" I stood clapping when Santa Claus rode off on his sleigh thinking it was over. But the man took my arm gently and said, "It is not over yet."

I sat down and watched as they brought Christ into Christmas by showing the Living Nativity. It was a perfect ending and brought tears to my eyes.

As I entered the darkening streets still filled with bustling people, I realized that my previous perception of New York City had been wrong. I asked a total stranger on the corner if I could use his cell phone to report to my busy husband. The man looked at me in surprise and said, "Sure." I smiled and thanked him. The streets were now bright with lights and the air was cool and crisp as I walked back down 5th Avenue.

My thoughts went back to the beginning of the day when I felt reluctant about being alone in New York City. It made me wonder how many of us let our own fearful attitude keep us from all the blessings God has for us each day. I realized that going out with a smile and the right perception changed who I was and how others saw me. Thank you people of New York for making this special memory.

Where to Look, What to Say

Not long ago I was sitting next to a small delicate woman that was so proud of her age she started the conversation by saying this was her 80th birthday. We were sitting together at the theater watching the Jersey Boys. This lovely sweet lady was from New Zealand, and her family was celebrating in New York City.

As we chatted I asked her "Where are you staying? At the Sheraton Hotel" she answered. "My group and I are staying there as well," I explained. She then went on to ask me if I had seen the large group of people staying there that had many deformities and scars. "Oh," I proudly said, " I am with that group." I then gently put my hand on hers and explained that we are a group of burn survivors who meet once a year. There were 900 attendees, the largest group to ever attend. She then went on to say, "I want to say something to them and I don't want to look away, but I DON'T KNOW WHERE TO LOOK OR WHAT TO SAY."

Many times I hear people say the same thing about anyone who has a difference; and that can mean a wheelchair, obesity, or disfigurements. I am part of a special group of people that have differences. I am a burn survivor. The fortunate thing about me is that I can cover up my scars. I don't choose to hide because I am very proud of what I went through to just be alive.

My hidden burns as well as my outgoing and friendly nature allow uninjured people to freely inquire about what it is to be a burn survivor, what it was like to be burned, how it is to live with the scars, how our life has changed and what happened. Letting others know that we are just human beings, like them, and even though we look different, there is nothing to fear from talking to us, looking at our scars or being near us. Luckily, our group is in the minority, but it gives us a large platform to inform others about burn injuries.

My new friend asked so many questions and sincerely wanted to learn what to do when she was around someone with a difference. I was honored to share some tips with her. During the intermission we talked about where to look. So many times we are told, "the eyes are the windows to our soul." I believe that is true, but I find that their eyes are the first place to look whether someone has a difference or not. It seems to me it is an instant connection. Look into the person's eyes and just say "Hello." I went on to say, most of us would rather have someone ask us about our injury than stare and turn away. At least I would. I introduced her to my husband sitting on the other side of me. He lost the left side of his face in our accident and the fingers on his left hand. I had her practice shaking his hand, looking in his eyes and saying "Hello."

By the end of the performance, we had hugged goodbye, shared addresses, and we went in different directions to our hotel. As soon as I returned, many of my burned friends were in the lobby laughing and talking so of course I joined in. Not long afterwards, I saw my new little theater friend walking towards me calling out my name. Immediately, I thought, this is perfect she can practice some more. I introduced her to many of my friends, and she talked and laughed with us for an hour or so.

How many of us feel uncomfortable around people that are not like us? I know for many years I did until I was the one that was

136

different. After our accident I felt invisible. Everyone that looked at me either turned away or made comments. At first I was bandaged and in a wheelchair with a body brace. Then I had to wear what they call a "Jobst Garment" for two years for my burns. It has been a long difficult journey but one of the most rewarding experience of my life.

Please remember, none of us asked to be different. So the next time you see someone, please look in his/her eyes, smile, and say "Hello".

Published on Susan's blog http://susanlugli.blogspot.com/ January 2, 2010

Through The Eyes of Children

My four-year-old granddaughter, Sophia, excitedly pulled me into her preschool class announcing, "Mrs. Bowman come quick and meet my Grandma." Sophia had a sunny expression on her face as her two blonde ponytails bounced in the air. As the teacher approached, Sophia shouted aloud, "This is my GRANDMA and she is all fired up!" The teacher and I looked at each other with a puzzled look, not understanding what she was talking about. I looked down at her little hand in mine and noticed she was looking at the burn scars I had on my arms from a motor home accident several years previous. That is how she was introducing me to her teacher. As I explained it to Mrs. Bowman, I felt great joy that my granddaughter was so proud of my scars that made me look different.

I have four other grandchildren and they all look at our burn scars differently. They do not know us any other way. One day we were all eating Sunday dinner together, and our oldest grandson was sitting next to his grandpa. Sebastian was quiet as he put his hand on top of his Granddad's hand with four amputated fingers. Sebastian had a serious look on his face and said, "Grandpa, if you would take a nap everyday your fingers would grow back." It was such a loving thought we all wished were possible.

Our complete family of ten moved together to a ranch several years ago, allowing me to be with three of the grandchildren almost daily their entire lives. With three generations living together, we are able to help each other and learn the old and new ways of life. I believe it is every mother and grandmother's dream come true.

I did not know my grandparents, and my mother passed away when I was very young. I had no role models to follow, but I knew what kind of parent and grandparent I wanted to be. Having the joy of the Lord in my life was my direction. So our days are filled with fun and laughter and song.

Because we look different due to our scars, I have tried to teach my grandchildren how to handle disfigurements and handicaps of any kind. I am always proud when they just go up to the person and treat them like they would anyone else, instead of standing back, staring or making comments.

One-day five-year-old Giovanna and I went to lunch at Wendy's. There was an obese woman who sat at the table beside us. As she passed by, she noticed my pretty little granddaughter and said "Hello." Giovanna pressed close to me and did not answer.

I told her it was all right but also brought to her attention how pretty the lady was and that she had brilliant blue eyes. We must always look for the good in people I told her. Before I knew it, she turned around and looked at the lady and said, "You have beautiful blue eyes." The lady smiled and I noticed her whole countenance changed, as did my granddaughter's. As we left, we talked about the warm fuzzy feeling Giovanna had inside because she made someone with a difference feel very special.

My youngest granddaughter, Isabella, proudly shows her Grandpa off to her friends. She calls him the "show and tell Grandpa."

One day Isabella ran into the market when she saw her Grandpa's truck out in the parking lot. She started yelling, "Grandpa" as she dragged her new friend by the hand. There was her Grandpa in the deli section waiting with a big hug. After introducing her new friend she asked, "Grandpa, show her your glass eye!" She is proud to show off the difference in him. See what I mean by "Show and Tell?"

Mason is the youngest grandkid. He is four years younger than Isabella. All our grandkids think Mason is the baby. Many a fight has occurred over who is going to be with Mason.

Even though Mason is the youngest, he has been around people with differences the most of all our grandkids. Our daughter and Mason have attended many WBC (World Burn Conferences) with us. Our daughter sings for the organization. Mason was three when he first attended. At that time, he saw many different types of prosthetic devices and deformities. He was totally taken with the wonderful people who showed him a great deal of love. At first, he stood back and was not sure. But before I knew it, he was touching the hooks and asking how they worked. Recently, he was able to witness what he calls the "Star Wars" bionic hands. I see so much compassion in this little boy and great potential for his future.

I can go on forever telling little stories, but the most wonderful thing in the world is being a grandparent. I love to hear our grandchildren call out each day, "GRANDMA", as if they had not seen me for weeks. They always want to be with me. We play hide and seek in the tall mustard grass and swim in the pond on a warm sunny day. We ride up the mountain singing, "You are my Sunshine." At the end of the day they say, "Grandma, I love you." Life cannot be more wonderful!

The Jesus in Me

My arms reach out to hold someone unable to wrap their arms around me. My smile touches others with tears in their eyes because I don't quickly look away. "That is the Jesus in me." I sit next to a person without hands. I gently touch their smooth stumps and give them a smile. Not a word is spoken. The smiles and the touch give the love and encouragement that is needed for them to go on. "That is the Jesus in me."

Without the love of Jesus shining through, I too would pass by those who are different, trying not to look because they would make me feel uncomfortable. I was not sure what to say or do. Sometimes, we need to be reminded that in an instant we could be that person sitting in a wheelchair. Or the person burned without hands or a face could be someone we love. Many do not want to face that reality, so they look away.

What would Jesus do? He visited and touched the lepers walking through their dark, dreadful existence. Yes, parts of their bodies were missing and the smell was probably sickening, but He sought them out when others refused to look. He had no fear of catching what they had. How opposite from the way many of us treat people who are different. We act like they are contagious!

I am blessed to be a burn survivor and to have walked that long hard journey to recovery. I want to be a shining light for the Lord so others can see Him in me. I understand how people feel who have a difference. It was not easy for me to be around anyone I thought was not normal, whatever that is. I remember being seventeen and having

142

to visit the mental institution where my father was living. Hearing the moaning sounds and screams scared me. Going to the cafeteria with him and seeing people spit out their food into rags made me sick to my stomach. It broke my heart every time I had to leave him in that place.

For most of my adult life people with differences bothered me. When I was in an accident and terribly burned, I was given the opportunity to experience firsthand what this feels like. Now I was the one people avoided looking at. At the time I was in a body brace and wheelchair and felt invisible! Even I avoided looking in a mirror, or even a window, so I did not have to see my reflection. Those who cared for me got impatient with my slow recovery wanting to go on with their own lives. At that time, I could not imagine why Jesus let this happen. As I slowly got better, I wanted to help others not feel invisible. People facing obesity, scars, deformities, or lack of self-esteem needed to experience what I had because they felt invisible too.

Through my pain, I chose daily to allow the light of Jesus to shine through me. With each new day, His understanding and His light would shine brighter. I walked in many of their shoes and knew their feelings because I had been there too.

Jesus said, *"I am the Light of the World."* John 8:12, NASB. He walked in all of our shoes, and experienced every difficulty on the earth. He told us He would not give us anything that we could not handle. If we desired to be like Him, we should rejoice in every trial that comes our way. Let the Jesus in you shine brightly so others can see and experience Him living in you.

The Best Time in My Life

I looked at my friend in the middle of the parking lot of our large shopping mall. She looked puzzled at me as I said, "Where did you park the car?" We both thought for a minute, and she started to laugh. "You are so silly. Don't you remember? You drove today." We both started to laugh. Before we knew it, other women around us joined in. Since that day we have grown to know the parking security guy quite well. Whenever he spots us wandering around, he drives up to us with a huge smile on his face.

I have found since I have been in my midlife stage that life is more fun. I seem to laugh at myself more. Others around me seem to understand me better and tolerate me more. By the time you are my age, your marriage has ended or succeeded. Your children have grown up, left home, and are on their own, hopefully doing well. We still have our health and energy to enjoy life. Your financial state is usually balanced. That is, unless you spend your savings on trying to look good with plastic surgery. It seems to be acceptable to be a little fluffy and to have little lines appear whenever you smile.

I look in the mirror early in the morning, when I get ready for the day, but seem to avoid the mirror the rest of the day. My mind says, "You don't look too bad for an old girl." But looking at a picture tells me something totally different. "Who is she? That can't be me!"

Whenever I go on a shopping trip with my friend, we encourage each other when we try on clothes. While in the changing rooms, we close our eyes or turn our backs on the full-length mirrors and complement each other. The funny thing is my head says, "You are still 30," but my body says, "Get over it!"

Not long ago, we were getting ready to go on a trip. I had my list written with the things I still had to do. One of those errands was to get gas in the car. Of course, my mind was going a mile a minute when I pulled in and started to pump. The attendant started to talk to me, and I immediately had a new best friend. We laughed and carried on. In the background I heard the gas click off. I quickly said my goodbyes and jumped in the car. Oh my gosh! As I pulled out I felt this huge crash and heard a loud sound. Needless to say, the gas started squirting all over the place. I realized I had forgotten to take the hose out of the tank. I immediately turned the car off, and I could hear my new best friend screaming angrily at me. Funny how fast people can forget who their friends are! It was an expensive disaster. I have been very careful ever since that day.

I think this is the best time in my life. I have five grandchildren that I am privileged to see everyday. We laugh, have fun, and share our lives together. My entire family is healthy, and we are close in every way.

When I look back into the picture albums of my early years, I wonder why I was not happy with myself. I was never pretty enough, thin enough, or had the right clothes. Yet, the pictures I look back at were of a young woman, pretty, thin, and looking like she had the world by a string. Her outsides were perfect but her insides were sad and insecure.

Those pictures make me more determined to be happy now. I feel secure in myself even if now I am truly, heavier, older, and my face is filled with smiling lines. My insides shine with happiness. I always try to remember, life is 10% circumstance and 90% attitude. That is how I have chosen to live the rest of my life.

My Friend Dick

Webster defines the word "friend" as *"one attached to another by affection or esteem."* My like turned quickly to love not long after I met my friend, Dick. He was a short, stocky Italian man my husband invited out from Providence, Rhode Island to do business with us. My husband grew to love and trust our friend as a confident partner. Dick was trustworthy and always reliable. We all grew to be the best of friends.

After more than thirty years of friendship, Dick died from leukemia recently. One side of me was so grateful that he is finally at rest with his family in heaven, but the other side grieved his loss. When he told me that he would not win this battle and would die soon, I could not imagine our lives without him. At first I cried with sadness then, after the shock wore off, we just talked about the process he was going through. We spoke of all the memories we had shared, and the excitement of going to a better place. He never married. He always lived and cared for his mother following his father's death many years ago. Actually, he always cared for his entire family. As I think back, he has always cared for my emotional needs when my husband was not around.

I can't really believe he is gone. He was always there even though he was a continent away. All I had to do was pick up a phone. I do not have any bad memories only good ones. I need to share them because I never want to forget one of the kindest, gentlest, sweetest men I have ever known. He was an example for men of all ages to follow. Dick was a quiet, kind, and gentle spirit. I am truly a better person because of knowing him.

Our first meeting was at our ranch in Sebastopol California. Dick always said it was like going to the zoo when he was at our house. He remembers me yelling over the intercom for our son, Todd, then ten, to come into the house. We were having spaghetti for dinner. In those days I was very insecure about my entertaining skills. The next morning I tried to serve him day-old coffee. He was appalled, but my thought was "Why waste it?" He remembers Nikki being a quiet gentle soul compared to the rest of the family. She could have been his child.

Not long after, he started the insurance company in Providence, Rhode Island for Rusty. We went back and forth for years, and with every visit, we relaxed with Dick. He had a beach house in Narragansett on the ocean where we spent many days. For a while he had a sailboat that we all enjoyed. Dick had tons and tons of books laying everywhere in both his houses, polo shirts, and baseball hats of every color. We used to go down to the wharf early in the morning when the fishing boats would come in and buy lobsters right off the boats. He loved to cook and would make me stay in the kitchen while the poor little lobsters were screaming to get out of the boiling water. I felt so badly for them, but he just laughed. Many a game was played in the kitchen of that house.

We would take the ferryboat over to Block Island and ride bikes around. We rented a pink Cadillac convertible to drive on Martha's Vineyard. In summer we would go out to the stock theater by the sea. I can only remember the one play that has the "Feed Me" plant, but I can't recall the name. It was great times. We would go to Newport to walk around the shops and see the big mansions.

He came our way to visit often. He was in Monterey with us when Rusty first got his new 1988 black Porsche. We had to take a ton of pictures of him in it so he could show it off when he got back home. Of course, he said it was his. We took trips up to Lake Tahoe in the winter. There he had a fall on his bottom that hurt his tailbone. He was in bad shape for a while, but we laughed through it all.

Rusty and our attorney were flying a small plane back east to see Dick on a business trip. The plan was that I was to fly out commercially and meet them with Dick. The night before I was to go, I had a dream that the small plane crashed, and they were killed. It scared me to death. All the way to Providence, I imagined the worst. I pictured Dick arriving to pick me up and having to tell me the bad news. When he arrived very late, I jumped to the conclusion he didn't know how to tell me. When I saw Dick I ran to him crying and begging him to tell me the bad news. Of course, he didn't know what I was talking about and why I was hitting him in the shoulder. After I calmed down, I could finally tell him. Oh how we laughed! From that point on he called me the "The Widow Lugli."

When Rusty and I separated, Dick was a rock for me. I called him many late nights just to talk. I trusted his advice knowing he loved us both. I took a trip to see him the beginning of the summer. We both had signed up for a Vermont bike ride in the fall. When I got off the plane, he told me he had a surprise for me at the beach house. It was hard for me as before I was always with Rusty when I went there. Now I felt alone. When we arrived at the house, he told me to shut my eyes and led me to a brand new bike! Dick and I rode all around the island every day getting in shape for the big ride. We would stop every now and then, sit on the rocks, and talk about plans for both our futures. We could talk about anything. Rusty was in a legal case in Philadelphia, so Dick drove me there to meet him. It was a confusing time, but we got through it.

That following month I went on a singles' cruise out of Florida and Dick had flowers delivered to my cabin. He always made me feel that everything would be all right. I knew he always cared. Just what I needed!

In the fall we did take our big ride. I flew out and we drove to Vermont. What a good time that was. I admired Dick for going, although I didn't give him much choice. He was a real trooper. Most of the other people were couples and we had a good time keeping them guessing about our relationship. We would kiss in the morning, spend the day together, kiss at night, and go to our own rooms. Rusty and I were working on our marriage at the time, so he sent me flowers and Dick a bottle of wine. You should have heard the talk the next day. It was so funny. One of the longest days was sixty miles and Dick came in last. I stood in the driveway while he rode real slowly towards me. I was humming "Chariots of Fire." Dick was tone deaf and when I would sing in the car he would hum, AWFUL. It would sound like a … I can't even describe it. IT WAS JUST AWFUL!!

After our accident in 1993, we didn't see Dick for a while. I know he was scared to see our burns knowing we almost lost Rusty. It took a couple of years to get back on our feet. When we did finally, we started to go to Boston for plastic surgery on Rusty's face. Dick would pick us up and take us to the hospital in Cambridge. We always stopped at the market place first to buy seafood. The following morning, Rusty would have surgery and stay one night. Then Dick would take us home with him to rest for a week. I so appreciated his support and company. I know Rusty did too. We made this same trip several times a year for three years. During that time we would take trips to Maine to see other islands in the area. There was always laughter and sometime tears during those years.

I remember when Dick got us tickets for the Phantom of the Opera in Boston. It wasn't long after we were burned, and I wasn't used to people staring at us. I cried through the whole play, and people commented about Rusty's mask during intermission. When Dick picked us up afterwards, I hit him and said, "How could you want us to see that awful play." Poor guy, he didn't have any idea what I was talking about. I felt so badly.

While Rusty and I were staying at Dick's beach house, our son, Todd, wanted me to fly to Florida to help his wife Gena take our two young grandkids to Bogotá, Colombia where they were moving for a year. Rusty just had surgery, and I didn't want to leave him to travel back to California by himself. I ended up going. After staying in Bogotá for three weeks and watching the revival going on there, I returned to Boston where my friend, Dick, once again picked me up. I recall going to a little restaurant across the street from a church that was dark and closed. I told Dick all about my stay and how all the people wanted church so badly that they would meet anywhere or any time. It made me cry to see how dark that church was in Boston when people in Columbia were so desperate to go to church.

Dick and I respected each other's faith. He called me a Holly Roller with my "Amen's." He was a good Catholic. One of the last times we were together, we went to a Catholic church on Fire Island. I wasn't too sure when to sit down, stand up, or anything else. He went forward for Communion and I followed. The Priest would put a wafer on your tongue. I thought, "How hard can that be?" Dick went first then he waited for me. I had my tongue out as I walked up to the priest so he could put the wafer on it. I noticed the priest had a funny look on his face. Dick started to laugh and whispered in my ear, "You just stuck your tongue out at the priest." How did I know?

Through those wonderful thirty years, we all shared good times and bad, but we all did it together. We saw many miracles and watched each other grow older. I will never have a friend like Dick again in my lifetime. I am honored to have known and loved him. We will all be together again someday. For now, I miss my friend.

Old Friends

I sobbed uncontrollably as we drove away from our home in Sacramento, California. The year was 2000, and we were moving to a new area six hours away from where we had lived in for sixteen years. It was a new beginning, but it was difficult leaving all my friends in the old neighborhood. Many of these friends were older women, and they had walked many different seasons along side of me.

I was thirty-eight when we moved into this old beautiful community. We had shared my son's drug addiction, my own marriage separation after twenty-five years, and then one year later, our renewal vows. Two years later we had a tragic accident that left my husband and me severely burned. That was a long journey and these ladies stayed right beside me for a year of recovery. They were always my encouragers and cheerleaders. Now we were moving into a new stage in our lives.

In 1990 Beryl and I started a Bible study. Beryl was my spiritual mother from the neighborhood. In the beginning, there were seven women - Joan, Diane, Chris, Vi, Vienna, Beryl and myself. This group grew as years went by, and now we are a total of seventeen, counting me. More than two decades later, we are all still together studying God's word every week. I am still blessed to have them in my life. Many of us talk often and I am always invited to special occasions. There is many a birthday party where the phone is passed around so I can be part of the celebration-- not in body, but in spirit. We are family!

For as long as I can remember, all of us gathered for a three or four-day retreat. When I lived near them, we would have the retreat in Lake Tahoe. Each year we would have a title and a Bible study pertaining to it. We studied "Women of the Bible", where each of us dressed and acted out our character. Other topics included "His Banner Over Me is Love", and "Personalities". We laughed till our stomachs hurt. Now we have our retreat at my new house near Santa Barbara. We studied "Growing Older Positively."

Miriam is eighty-nine years old and has never missed a retreat. She teaches me so much about being a gentle spirit full of grace. Each lady has her own unique gifts to share.

Ruthy, one of my wonderful sisters, was graduated from college recently. I went to Sacramento to attend her celebration party with all the Bible study girls. She has studied faithfully for the past ten years to get her degree while working full-time. We are all so proud of her.

As I looked around the table, I saw the wisdom of the years on their beautiful faces and realized they still have so much to teach me. I have absorbed much through the past years and look forward to many more years with them. Even with the graying of their hair and wrinkles on their faces, they laugh like schoolgirls when we are all together. Each morning when I awaken, I thank God for these women in my life. In the darkening shadows of their lives their integrity sparkles like a diamond in the sand.

Depression

"Low in spirits; dejected, disheartened." That is how Webster defines "depression". What can create this horrible feeling? Our circumstances certainly can. But what if nothing is wrong and you just feel crummy?

That is what is going on with me right now. I have prayed about the feelings, but nothing has happened yet. I have gone through everything in my life and thanked God for my physical and emotional situation. I have asked forgiveness and repented for the things I needed to. This is a day where I can't figure out what my feelings are. I feel tired, hungry, and negative. It is hard to explain. My head feels blank and my body old and tired.

My husband took me away this week overnight, just to get away. It was all right. We had a nice time, but I actually felt quite bored.

We are preparing for a big trip, and that isn't even exciting me. Chocolate hasn't helped. I ate a full can of frosting mix over the past two days. I am now eating protein to see if that does the trick. I have been good about going to Curves to work out three times a week. I have gone out of my way to visit people in need. I am doing everything I tell others to do when they are depressed! I know what. I will go take a walk in the mud to see if that helps. This awful feeling didn't go away, but the walk did help for the moment. I know what to do! I will play some Christian music. I am sure that will help!

I always tell others, "It takes one to know one." That could be in any circumstance we are in. So, my question to myself is, "How can I understand other's depression if I don't experience it myself?" Well, here I am in the midst of it. I pray this too shall pass! FAST!

Not A Coincidence

As I turned the key to open the door at the Mt. Herman Conference Grounds Hotel, I felt nervous to meet my new roommate. I had not shared a room with someone that I did not know in a very long time. My son had planned to attend the writer's conference with me but at the last minute canceled out.

I slowly opened the door only to find the room empty. On one side of the room was a suitcase neatly placed in the corner. A special pillow and blanket lay on the bed while a small picture frame was placed on the side table. My mystery roommate was not there so I quietly picked up the picture and viewed a lovely woman, about my age, and a handsome man standing next to her.

I put my belongings away in the dresser drawers and placed my suitcase next to the dresser. I was anxious to get checked into my classes and collect my syllabus in the hospitably room.

This was the second writer's conference I had gone to and certainly the largest. There were about three hundred participants sitting in the large chapel waiting excitedly for instruction for the next four days. I did not know a single soul so I talked freely to those around me. After our first meeting, I walked slowly out to the courtyard for our break time. I was talking to a newfound friend when a tall slightly red curly haired woman approached me. She had a large smile on her face as she said, "Sue Lugli, you are my roommate!" The enthusiasm in her voice made me feel like I was someone special. I quickly looked down at her nametag and responded, "Oh Priscilla. I look forward to getting to know you." She started to laugh and said, "I already know you." I knew I must have looked puzzled at her comment. I had met so many new people during the past ten years. Her face was not familiar. Since our accident a decade prior, I had been speaking and writing about our incident to many groups throughout the United States.

I felt embarrassed to ask, "How do you know me?" It was then that she started to explain our meeting. "Well," she stated, "I met you in October 1998 at a woman's retreat in Lake Tahoe. You spoke about the story you wrote in *"Today's Christian Woman"* magazine, called "Out of the Fire." I talked to you afterwards about my own accident and the pain I was in. You even prayed with me. Afterwards, you encouraged me to write my own story. I did, and that is why I am here at this conference."

I stood stunned for a moment. The realization of how important our words are to each other and what a difference we make in each other's lives began to register. I had no idea all those years ago what an impact my words would have on this lovely lady.

I now see God's plan. The things that first seemed like obstacles, God had turned into opportunities to share His love with others.

This reunion was a "divine coincidence" to renew a relationship and to see how God works in all things.

The Painting

Early in the morning, I sit with a cup of hot tea in my living room in my comfortable chair. As the sunlight shines through the large window behind me, I watch the colors change on the painting hanging over my fireplace. It is a large 32x32" canvas with a 4" gold frame surrounding it. The bright oranges, purples, blues, whites, and browns melt together into a collage of color.

I remember the day my cousin, Phyllis, called from Ohio to talk to me in the hospital. I had been severely burned in an accident, and it was a struggle to tell her the details. The pain was so extreme. All I can recall doing is crying. She kept repeating, "It will be all right."

Later that week she shared my ordeal with her daughter, Lesley. Lesley was a gifted artist. As she listened to the details of my accident, she was once again reminded of her great fear of fire. Later that evening, Lesley started to paint with her mind filled with what her mother had told her earlier. With her contrast style of painting, each brush stroke was filled with color and emotion. The hours sped by quickly. Lesley looked at her work and whispered, "I will finish in the morning." Exhausted from emotion, she fell asleep and started to dream. Images of the design and brilliant colors swam in her head as an image of a woman appeared. Morning came too soon. As she passed by the colorful canvas, she was stopped by what she saw. The image of the woman she saw in her dream was in her painting. She said quietly, "It is finished."

That painting leaned against a wall in Lesley's house for many months before her mother, Phyllis, saw it. After Lesley told her about the night she painted it, my cousin called to tell me she thought the painting should be mine. Soon a photo arrived for me to approve. I immediately made arrangement for it to be sent to me in California.

When the painting arrived, I just saw a mass of colors and a faint image of a woman. She was standing sideways looking at an orange color that resembled a head of a wolf. I had this unusual piece of art framed and hung it on the living room wall.

At first as I passed it, that was all I could see with my eyes. It hung for several months before my daughter noticed something more. She said, "Mom, Jesus is shielding the woman from the flame." As she pointed out His image, I could see what she was talking about. There was Jesus' face looking down at the woman with His arms outstretched and His flowing gown separating her from the fire. Behind the woman to the side of Jesus were three crosses reminding me that He died for me.

Many others have sat and looked at this divinely painted work of art. They have seen other images like an angel kneeling behind the woman with her wings spread wide.

Lesley allowed God to flow through her talented hands, that night. I wondered if she was totally aware.

How often in our lives we see only the jarring colors that reflect our own pain and the pain of others. Only when I looked at the painting through my own healing eyes did I see the true picture.

Written in loving memory of my second cousin Lesley. Thank you for sharing your gift.

The Aching Heart of Mary

Mary knew at the beginning that her son Jesus was different. She also knew He did not belong to her. At the age of twelve Jesus said, *"Did you not know that I must be about My Father's business?"* Luke 2:49, NKJ. She and Joseph were human. They must have felt a stab of pain and rejection at those words. Like all mothers, we try to protect our children. As Jesus grew, He was not accepted. As an adult, the majority rejected Him. Mary knew there would be a sad ending.

I could relate. My son was one of my biggest challenges. I knew from the beginning that Todd was different. He was extremely hyperactive and was not accepted by anyone but me. At times, even I found it difficult to be with him. I called myself his protector and security blanket. Teachers would not have him in their classes unless I volunteered a day or two a week. My life was his for most of the first eighteen years of his life.

I tried to prepare for an empty nest. A couple of years before he was eighteen, I signed up for college classes and thought about what I would do when he left. When my children were young, I read a prayer how our children are not our own. When I prayed, I always started my prayer by thanking God for loaning me His children to raise for Him. Many times I would ask, "Are you sure Lord you sent my son to the right family?" But then I would remember the verse that says, *"God will not allow any difficulty to come into our lives that we are not capable of bearing."* I Cor. 10:13 - my version. I was always grateful for the Lord's confidence and encouragement. Many times I felt like giving up, but I would claim this verse and live by it. The Lord also kept reminding me *"Train up a child in the way he should go, and when he is old he will not depart from it."* Proverbs 22:6, NKJ.

One of the hardest times was his senior year in high school when he started using drugs. We had to ask him to leave our home. Todd was eighteen, a legal age to be responsible for himself. My heart was broken. I did not realize until this time how much he had consumed of my life. Every time I looked at our family photos in the hall, I would mourn his loss. At night, I would wake with fear that he would take his own life. We went through both inpatient and outpatient drug rehab with him. This process was valuable to his father and me, but didn't seem to help him. I knew we did the best job of raising him we knew how. So I hung on to God's Word. At times I would have to scream out loud, "You said you would not give us more than we can handle! You must think we are super people!" Those five years were difficult for me. Our business suffered. My husband found the company of someone else more appealing, so we were separated. My heart was aching from the loss. Our daughter was away at school, and I found my solace in being with her occasionally. My Heavenly Father and I were the family now. I found complete peace in Him. My knees were ruby red from being on them and praying for my husband and children. I claimed His promises over and over.

After those five years of lessons learned, the sun started to shine again. My husband and son took a trip by themselves to Australia where they both struggled with their demons. My husband finally accepted Christ as his Savior and Todd gave up drugs for alcohol. By the end of the trip, he gave up alcohol to renew his relationship with Jesus. Talk about answer to prayer!

We rejoiced when they returned, but there was much work to be done rebuilding our relationships. The Lord had sent a lovely girl into Todd's life while he was away at school. She loved the Lord and wanted to serve Him. By this time, so did Todd. The Lord did deliver my son totally from drugs and alcohol and gave him a new life. You can't get much better than that. Within six months they were married and off to another state to attend Bible college.

In the meantime, my husband and I were starting over after twenty-five years. For the first time Christ was the center of our marriage, and I was the happiest girl alive. My dreams were coming true and my prayers had been answered.

By the time two years had passed, Todd and Gena were expecting their first baby. Todd was working and going to school in Texas planning to be in the ministry. All I could think about was my first grandchild. My life had been children, and now I was having my own grandchild. Rusty and I would lie in bed and dream about the day this baby would be born and all the things we would do as long distance grandparents.

Our daughter, Nikki, had always been our sunshine, and she lived near to us. Todd had demanded so much of our energy most of his life, we were enjoying our time with her now. Life seemed very good.

Two years and five months after we renewed our vows, our life changed once more. Rusty, Nikki, and I were in a horrendous accident where we were all severely injured and burned. Once again I had to believe that the Lord does not give us more than we can handle. This time I said many times to Him, "Are you sure?" My heart was not just aching but breaking with sadness for our entire family. We had come so far, but now more lessons to learn. Do you ever want to just say, "When is it enough?" Todd and Gena arrived with just a few months before the baby was to be born. We hung between life and death. Our daughter's back was badly broken. I don't know how life could be gloomier. We did live, but it took five years to be put back together again. The journey of a burn injury is long and painful. Now we proudly carry our scars as a badge of courage. We have all learned many lessons through this experience.

As anniversaries of the accident come and go, I look back over this time as one of growth in our inner beings. I realize that God's Word is alive and true. *"For nothing is impossible with God."* Luke 1:37, NIV. *"I can do everything through him who gives me strength."* Phil 4:13, NIV.

Like Mary, I have seen much heartache as a mother, a wife, and a person experiencing physical pain.

God has answered my prayers in making my son His own and giving Todd the desire to serve Him. Todd now seeks to bring others to a personal relationship with Christ. My heart is proud that he has a wife who wants the same thing.

My daughter-in-law and I have grown together over the past decade, answering another prayer of mine. My Bible study girls and I would pray for a Naomi and Ruth relationship. And that has happened. My son and his wife have honored me with four beautiful grandchildren. My daughter Nikki has honored me with my grandson, Mason. I have also been blessed with having them live within half a mile from me for five years. The last two granddaughters and grandson, I have seen almost every day of their lives.

The first two years of the five my husband and I lived in Sacramento where I worked with burn patients at Shriner's and University of California at Davis hospitals speaking as an advocate on their behalf. The past three years we have all lived together on a ranch in Central California, and I am full time grandma. I have loved my new life, but it has been challenging also. I think at times when God was forming me in my mother's womb He said, "Let's call her challenger." I say to that, "Thanks God. You know what will keep me on my knees."

My biggest joy in my life is my grandchildren. The desire of my heart has been to make a difference in their lives. I know once again that they are not mine. They are the Lord's and He will care for them. When my son said to me "I must get about my Father's business," I knew that it meant he would be leaving our ranch to pursue overseas missions with his family. I am so proud of Todd and know my prayers have been answered. Like Mary, I KNOW I was just a vessel for God to use. The Lord is now using my son to give His message to others.

Little Church on the Ranch

Our son returned from a mission's trip to India and announced that the Lord told him to start a new church in our valley. When God spoke, we listened! At the time, he was working as a youth pastor at a local church. We were enjoying having the youth at our ranch paint balling, having retreats, and other great activities. Now, with God's Word in his head, it was time for a change.

We had just finished putting up a huge Quonset hut. We built a room attached in the front of it to resemble an old Western hotel. As the family stood admiring the two-story building, you could almost see the horses tied to the railings and hear laughter coming from within. Beside it was an old tin building with a false front and a sign saying "Wells Fargo Bank" Another building said, "Blacksmith." Right in front of it was a covered wagon. On the other side of the old hotel was the bunkhouse with a sign that says, "Grandchildren Welcomed." Our little western town complete, it was time to now decide what to do with the old hotel. My husband said, "It will be perfect place to display my old cars." Our daughter who loves Karaoke and dancing said, "What a great dance hall." Our son stood tall and said, "It is God's house - our new Church." Guess who won?

The little church on the ranch began. We met every Friday night at 7:00 with people from different churches who came from all the communities in the valley. At first it was a few, then the church grew rapidly to about fifty or sixty people. The local casino donated old bingo chairs giving each person a comfortable seat. Even though they were pink, we appreciated them. Each week I made sure the building was clean and made brownies and lemonade. Our son preached most nights and our daughter-in-law led worship. We had several others playing drums and guitars.

One night my son had a special speaker from out of town come. Henry and his wife stayed in the bunkhouse for the weekend. He loved Max, my German shepherd. Max was his best friend. I'll never forget the look on my son's face when Henry told him that he would not preach unless Max was right next to him up front. My children did not like animals in the building. Somehow, they always came in, like it or not!

It was wonderful! I would sit and watch older ladies petting cats that wandered in and kids with big dogs sleeping at their feet. You could see the sun set through the big window and hear horses whinnying out in the pasture. Several times a bird or two would get caught flying around in the big Quonset hut.

This little church continued for a year or so until we out-grew it and moved to town. It was lovely seeing all different denominations meet together in unity on common ground. I believe the ranch was a place we all could meet and not feel guilty about Sunday morning church. It was a place to be with other Christians and share the love of the Lord.

The main element was always there - Jesus never missed a Friday night.

Spooky

MEOW-MEOW was the only sound I heard in the pitch-black darkness of the night. As I sat up in my bed with sleepy eyes, I could see the silhouette of our black slender kitty sitting in the flower box outside our window. She was making an announcement that our door was closed to HER bedroom. At four o'clock in the morning, she was ready to come to bed. I usually left the door open for her convenience to come in her kitty door when she felt like coming home. I got up quietly and opened the door and went back to bed. Within minutes I could feel a little thump on the bed as she curled up in her favorite spot. The next morning, while she was still fast asleep, my husband and I laughed at how smart she was and how she always got our attention.

Spooky was our favorite cat. There was always excitement around when she was in the room. We moved to the country from the city a few years back, and she adjusted splendidly. She was small in size. Her black fur was shiny and sleek with about six white hairs on her chest. I noticed a little piece of her ear missing similar to a bite being taken out of it. After all, she was the GREAT BLACK HUNTER.

Many a late night snack would be had in our bathroom bathtub. We would be awakened by the sounds of a squeaking mouse running circles in our tub. After about an hour of fun, a very satisfied cat would jump on our bed for a good night's sleep. We never knew what remains we would find in the morning from her nightly catch. There were times in the middle of the day when I would enter our room and find a little bird flying around. It felt I lived in a zoo! All five grandchildren would run around trying to catch the very frightened bird. Not long ago, I was lying in bed looking out the window and saw a large lizard climbing up our curtain. As we all know, lizards are the fastest things on four legs. But our cat is faster.

Our daughter Nikki rescued Spooky as a tiny kitten from the vet where she worked. At first we weren't sure we needed another cat. We already had a white cat that my husband loved. But how could anyone resist a cute little black kitten with big brown eyes? It did not take long for our white cat to get her nose out of joint. She soon adopted our neighbors as her new family, and we were once again a one-cat family. As Spooky grew, we started noticing some of her favorite behaviors. Every night she would find a lap or leg to lie on. She would stretch out with all four paws hanging over our leg. She preferred not to be touched. I always said she was a "Hang in there kitty."

When the children arrived, Spooky disappeared into her hiding place under the bed. Our large German shepherd, Max, grew up with Spooky. They learned to respect each other and became very good friends. The difference in size did not matter; they had an understanding for each other. I would even hire a house sitter to just stay with Spooky so she wouldn't be lonely while we were gone.

A few years ago, I was doing my monthly duty by putting on their flea medication. My mind was scattered, as usual, and I put the dog medicine on the cat by mistake. Within a few hours I found Spooky on the bathroom floor shaking uncontrollably with blood drooling out of her mouth. It scared me to death. I wrapped a towel around her and held her tightly in my arms. We quickly took her to the vet where her life was saved. I felt so guilty for so long. Rusty would kid me about it unmercifully.

Spooky has been a huge part of our lives. We enjoyed laughing and talking about her for hours. But she has not come home to her nightly bed for days, and we miss her. I am not sure where she is or what has happened to her.

A few weeks ago we brought two new kittens home. We needed more cats to help take care of the mice problems in the barn. I remembered how our white cat reacted when we brought Spooky home, and I was concerned about it. I thought we were being very careful about the attention we were giving to the new kittens. I am afraid Spooky said, "No way Jose," and found another home.

We miss seeing our beautiful black feline stretch her long limbs and say MEOW to us in the morning. I would do anything to have her back in our lives.

Like all things in life, they have a season. I know the Lord gives and Lord takes away. We have had many animals in our many years of marriage, but this little black kitty will always be first on our list.

Hormone Madness

As I read an article in Time magazine about "Hormone Therapy," it started to make me think about getting off my hormone treatment I had been on for the past fifteen years. I felt confused. Some experts say its good, and some say it's bad. I had tried one time before, but gave up after a few weeks.

This time I said to myself, "I CAN make it." Over the next month I weaned myself off my estrogen. Within a short time I started experiencing the almighty hot flashes, especially at night while I lay awake with insomnia. The horrible memories from my past started to invade my mind. "I CAN do this," I said once again. I worked extra hard during the day so I would be good and tired at night. I even put a cool rag and baby power next to my bed. My husband tried to support me in this mission, but there was a small problem. He had sleep apnea and required a CPAP machine with a mask that has two holes on the side.

We were both asleep when the hot flash attacked me. I was in a cold sweat and grabbed for the baby powder. As I was putting it all over me I suddenly heard my poor husband coughing and struggling for air. It wasn't a pretty picture! Soon I realized that the safe way to get through this time was to sleep in separate beds. That worked for a short time until I began sleeping only three hours a night. I had the cleanest house in the neighborhood, but I was exhausted. Once again I said, "I CAN! this is not going to beat me."

A few days later our friends invited us out to a buffet one evening. I hadn't seen them since I started this mission to clean up my system. I had worked extra hard on my face that night and made my makeup just right. The first thing my friend wanted to know was why I had dark circles under my eyes and my skin seemed so dry. I had noticed that my face needed extra moisturizer lately. The crevices seemed to resemble a cracked shell on a hard-boiled egg. Oh my, others noticed my changes also. As we stood in the long line waiting to be served, I started to tell my estrogen-taking friend about my venture. I noticed my voice being louder than usual, and I seem to be irritated with everyone around me. Suddenly, the single lady in front of us turned around and said, "You poor thing. You need to get back on your estrogen." How dare she tell me what I needed! Immediately, I started to yell at her. Since I am usually nice to everyone, whether I like them or not, I could not believe my behavior.

Six weeks had passed and I was still saying, "I CAN do this." Now everyone around me had a clean house, my circles were darker under my eyes, and my face drank moisturizer three times a day. I wasn't too nice to be around, but my family was trying to support me. I just needed a little more time.

A few days later my grandchildren had their spring concert at school. I thought this was just the ticket I needed to lift my spirits. Mason, my two-year-old grandson, accompanied me to the school to watch the other four grandchildren perform. Weeks before I had learned how to prepare for the hot flashes that seemed to invade me, I'd tuck handy wipes in my purse and a sweater that I could remove. We were sitting in the second row enjoying the performance of my darling grandchildren, Sophia 11, Sebastian 12, Giovanna 8 and Isabella 6, when the invasion hit.

I quietly took Mason's hand and led him to the back of the room. We stood by the wall, and I took off my sweater and started to fan myself with the program. I looked at Giovanna who was standing on the stage. She was the one granddaughter who had always understood me with great compassion. She immediately took her little hands and held them to her heart silently saying, "Oh poor Grandma!." I couldn't believe it! Even she knew what was going on with me. Within seconds a lady standing next to me tapped me on the shoulder and pointed down to my grandson, Mason. He was standing in front of me with his shorts pulled down to his feet and his t-shirt pulled up around his neck! How could this be? Even the two-year-old felt sorry for me. I told myself, "That's it! I couldn't stand it any more!" This was the last straw for me.

I take my hat off to those who have beaten the habit of taking estrogen. I lasted eight weeks. But I can honestly say, "This girl will probably be on hormones until the day I die." I have a feeling that another article will come along and once again give me the desire to try to get off estrogen some day. For now, I seem to be the nice person I try to be. I am getting the sleep I need. And my husband and I are sleeping together in the same bed again. Thank God!

We Made Cookies

I have been trying to make my six-year-old grandson, Mason, aware that the United States of America is in a war in Iraq. I have several young men that I know who are over there. We have been making and sending cookies to them. Mason's job was to put two cookies in a small zip lock bag for each soldier. I kept telling him that it makes our soldiers feel good to receive something from home so they know they are not forgotten.

This year Mason was able to go to the World Burn Conference with us in New York City. We changed planes at the Colorado Airport. During our layover, I noticed many young men and women in uniform. I looked down at Mason and said, "There is one of the soldiers who fights for our freedom. Let's go thank them." He followed close behind me and watched as I put my hand out. Each young woman and man shook my hand. I quickly responded, "Thank you for fighting for my freedom. This is my grandson, Mason." He looked at them and then at me as I repeated "Thank them for your freedom." He quietly looked them in the eye and said, "WE MADE COOKIES."

I was so proud but a little confused, as were the soldiers. I then remembered the cookies that we had been sending. I bet this little boy felt that each one of these soldiers had eaten one of our cookies. I then explained to these brave soldiers. Many actually said, "They were the best cookies they ever ate." Mason felt good about his way of helping fight this horrible war.

My Heartbeat

"Thump, thump" was an unfamiliar sound to me. Usually, all I heard was the wheezing sound of my breath. Each breath increased the strain on my heart.

Webster defines the word "heart" as, "The hollow, muscular organ in vertebrates that receives blood from the veins and pumps it into the arteries by regular, rhythmic contractions." Or, "The heart considered as an emotional center as a mood or disposition."

My heart journey began when I was eight years old. My mother had hardening of the arteries. My early memories were of my mother having difficulty breathing. She was always tired. I remembered my parents sitting at the kitchen table talking about the possibility of my mom being one of the first persons to have open-heart surgery. Doctors said she had only a 50/50 chance of surviving. My parents chose not to risk it and Mother died not long after.

All my life I have been aware of this cursed family history. Absolutely everyone on my mother's side of the family had heart disease. I was confronted with this fact when I traveled to the East Coast in 1990 to renew my relationship with my mother's side of the family. The only surviving member was her sister who was seventy-three years old. Two weeks later my last remaining aunt died. All my other cousins had already died from a heart condition. I thought, "How strange when we have come so far in our medical field." I have always taken good care of myself with yearly checkups, eating and exercising right, never smoking or drinking. I was determined that heart disease would never get me!

As I sat and wrote about my feelings, I looked down to see the beautiful heart shaped paperweight I was presented last week for speaking at a conference in Canada. Little did I know then, that a week later I would be in the hospital undergoing a test to tell me that my main heart artery was 99% clogged!

Tears streamed down my face as I watched the angioplasty procedure on the small screen next to me. All I kept thinking was, "I thought I would beat this!" But I didn't. I watched the small wire enter my artery and push the plague away. It formed a space for the balloon to expand the artery and allow the blood to rush through again. It was like a miracle watching the blood make a path to my heart. I could hear the sound of the blood flowing and my heart beating. As I watched carefully I realized that "Heart disease did not beat me!" I was alive by the grace of God.

I had some strange feelings and emotions the week after this heart procedure. My breathing got better and I could truly hear my heart beat. I was very aware that my blood was flowing by the color in my cheeks and my body saying, "It was OK to rest and get ready for a new season God has prepared for you." I seem to cry easier and not take a second of my life for granted. I am blessed to have a wonderful doctor, family, and friends who are walking beside me in this recovery. They are watching me be all that God has planned for me.

Breath of Life

Did you ever wonder how one event in your life can change the rest of your life? As I thought back over the past months, I am in awe of how events were occurring now because of something that happened to me over a decade ago.

I kept my head down as I crawled away from the burning motor home I was traveling in. I could not see ahead of me because of the billowing black smoke and the intense heat. My thoughts were, "I must be in Hell." All I could see was liquid pouring off my arms and legs. At the time I did not know it was my skin melting from the heat. With each breath, I inhaled, a burning pain pierced my throat.

A few years ago we moved to a manufactured home in a new valley where the fields are beautiful and the harvest is plenty. We can see the wondrous mountains all around us for miles and miles. I felt all my dreams had come true. I woke up each morning with the sounds of tractors plowing the fields, animals greeting me, and my grandchildren laughing. How could life be any better?

The only problem was as soon as we moved there, I started having a problem with my breathing. With each gasp for breath, the wheezing sounds increased. After seeing many doctors and several trips to the emergency room, the diagnosis was asthma. Inhalers became a way of life for me, and I never left home without one. Many other medicines were added as my condition continued to get worse.

Finally, we decided to move off the ranch away from the beautiful fields that contained farm chemicals we felt might be creating my problem. We moved to a beautiful home a few miles away in town. But the problem continued and actually became worse.

Not only did my breathing become more labored, but also now chest pressure came along with it. How could this be happening? What was going on? Since we moved, all our wonderful friends came to visit. We were doing a lot of entertaining. With each speaking engagement, I became more drained and exhausted. The pressure was getting worse. Finally, I ended up in the emergency room. But all the tests results were negative.

The following day my Santa Barbara doctor ordered two tests. After putting a scope down my throat, he saw my trachea was hardly open. I urgently needed help. The next test was a chemical stress test at the hospital. During that test, I went into cardiac arrest. What a day! My doctor immediately admitted me to the hospital. It was overwhelming news for a girl who hates hospitals and loves shopping. I was expecting company from New York the next day, and my car was full of food. HOW COULD I BE IN THE HOSPITAL? I HAD TOO MUCH TO DO! Isn't life funny?

Early the next morning a wonderful team of doctors did angioplasty on my 99% blocked artery. What an amazing procedure to open my blocked artery with a small balloon. Almost instantly, I had no more pressure. I seemed to breathe a little easier and my color was much better. I felt so much better with just that one procedure done. The next morning the same team put a bronchoscope down my throat to check my trachea. Soon after waking up, my doctor told me I had to wait two months before I would be sent to a Los Angeles hospital for a laser bronchoscopy and stent placement. THAT SOUNDED VERY SCARY!

Here is where the event that happened a decade and a half previously comes in. During the years after the fire, scar tissue grew around my trachea. For all the years I had trouble breathing, I was treated for asthma. My trachea was never checked. Who would think? I realized if you inhaled heat and smoke to a high degree, it can cause severe breathing problems later on. Doctors were so concerned with my painful burns healing they didn't go further to look at my difficult breathing. Although uncomfortable, my breathing problems became my normal way to life. I almost waited too long to get help.

After two months of letting my heart settle down and being on a blood thinner, it was finally time to take care of the next portion of my problem. I was sent to a specialist in Los Angeles where I had the throat procedure done in an outpatient clinic. Normally, the trachea was about the size of a quarter. But over a period of time mine had shrunk to less than a dime. My throat was now only 5% open. No wonder I struggled to catch each breath and wheezed constantly! I was very scared, but knew I had no other option. As soon as I woke up in recovery, I couldn't wait to talk to see how I would sound. There had been a chance my vocal chords would be damaged during the procedure. I looked up at the handsome young man that was pushing my gurney into the elevator. With a sleepy voice I said, "Do you hear that?" He looked at me like I was crazy and said, "What lady?"

My breathing was so quiet with no wheezing at all. I had a very sore throat for about a week, but that was it! I feel blessed with each and every breath I take. I am so grateful because the end of this story could have been very different if my doctors had not done those tests. Thank you Lord.

Be Still

"Be still and know that I am God."
Psalm 46:10a, NIV

One beautiful sunny day, I was working out in my garden. Life had changed completely for me in the past few months. My entire family of ten had moved three hundred miles away from the city to a ranch. Instead of a big beautiful house complete with gardeners, we were starting over with run down property and a manufactured home. Even though many would think, "What a dream come true!" Living with my husband, son and daughter, their spouses and five grandchildren was an adjustment.

Nearly a decade prior, my family was in a horrible accident that left my husband and me severely burned. At that time we all realized how fast our lives could change. We began working toward living together on a ranch.

During the past decade, I had jumped feet first into a new life as a burn survivor. As soon as I was physically able, I started working with other burn survivors to help them to be able to adjust to their new lives. I ran our local support group and spoke at burn retreats and conferences. I wrote our story, "Out of the Fire," that was published in *"Today's Christian Woman"* magazine. All of these experiences have been rewarding.

I realize that whatever circumstance in which I find myself, I bloom where I am planted. That is not a bad thing to do! However I know now I had kept myself so busy that I did not take time to think and heal from my own loss.

That season was a piece of the puzzle of my life. As I quietly pulled the weeds in my country garden, I thought back and wondered what God had in store for me now. I felt His voice ringing in my ears, saying, "Be still. Just be and not do." My entire life I had kept myself busy for all kinds of reasons. Do any of you relate? I loved to be productive and have accomplishments. But it kept me from thinking about my sad childhood, the loneliness I felt, the rejection I experienced, and the pain I had now from being different with my burn scars. Keeping busy helped me avoid dealing with the unbearable times in my life.

In the quiet surroundings of hundreds of acres, I was alone with God. I was able to hear that I had to now face my past. This was a time to be quiet and write my story. I began to see how God used events of my life as an opportunity to glorify Him. I believe sometimes we get stuck in certain seasons. I wonder if we are reluctant to go on with the next mainly because we do not know what is ahead of us.

We all have a story! It took moving from the busyness of my former life to this quiet valley to be still enough to hear God's voice. I had been so busy helping others through their burn injuries that I did not face my own fears. It became crystal clear one evening when I ended up in the hospital because I could not breathe. As I laid on the gurney waiting to be seen, looking up at the lights on the ceiling brought back horrible memories. My biggest fear was to not be in control of what was happening to me. Tears streamed from my eyes as I begged my family not to leave me.

Thinking back over the decades of my life, I know God has carried me through each circumstance and given me opportunities to share Him with others. During many turbulent times, I have called upon Him and relied on His help. God has always been faithful. I have not always been able to thank Him for all my circumstances. I now look at each one of them as another part of the puzzle that made me who I am today. I am a strong woman with confidence in my Lord. I feel honored to have been chosen to be His instrument. God says of the prophet Jeremiah, *"Before I formed you in the womb I knew you, and before you were born I consecrated you; I have appointed you a prophet to the nations."* Jeremiah 1:5, NAS. Until now, I never really understood that verse also applied to me. God knew me, consecrated me for His use, and appointed me before I was ever born.

This year of being still has given me an opportunity to see in a positive way every incident in my life has worked together for God's glory and good. As long as I walked the trials of my journey hand-in-hand with Him, He revealed His appointed assignment for me.

My garden flourishes now and our family has settled into a wonderful life style. I have the privilege of being part of my grandchildren's lives each day watching them grow along with my flowers. We are all blooming into God's perfect plan and the lesson I have learned is to be still and listen.

Divine Errors

"How many success stories have you heard lately?" Unfortunately, there are not many. Or at least we don't hear about them. Usually, we hear stories of heartbreak, divorce, and death through drug abuse or eating disorders. People need to know that a family can go through all of those situations, and more, and still come out at the end. It has always been my desire to encourage others that **"Nothing is Impossible."**

I wanted to put my short stories in one book to share our family's story, especially with my grandchildren. So I began looking for a publisher. I am not a perfectionist, but I knew what I wanted. I outlined the purpose of doing a book and how I wanted the short stories to flow, one after another. Each story had it's own lessons, and hopefully, the solutions I found would help a reader to change their life.

Just like my life, the lessons from this book adventure did not come easily or quickly. Sometimes I wanted to quit for all kinds of reasons. Writing is hard work! It was painful to remember back to sad memories. I would be reminded of so many lessons I had to learn and how many choices I had made in my life. Like everyone, my decisions were sometimes right, sometimes wrong. The key was I had to do something or get stuck!

I feel we have 3 choices in facing hard decisions:

1. We can go backwards and not learn anything.
2. We can stay where we are and not change.
3. We can move on, change and grow.

I spent many hours trying to find the right publisher to help me self-publish the book. Since I had never done anything like this before, I had a lot to learn.

When the book was finally published I realized it was not exactly what I wanted. There were many typos and mistakes not corrected in the final printed copy. As I read through the pages, I could see the errors that needed to be corrected, but it was too late.

With each book I sold, I would hear little comments like, "Oh Sue, I am sorry but there are two page 60's." Sure enough when I checked there were two page 60's. Oh my gosh! People handed me lists of what was wrong or returned the book with Post-it notes marking each error. After many more people offered helpful reminders that there were mistakes, I really didn't know what to say. But I knew I had a choice how I responded.

One Sunday after church a sweet lady came up to me and said that she had really enjoyed reading my book. Then she whispered, "I am almost done, but you know, there are a few problems with the book." At that point I found myself saying, "You know, I already know that. What I want you to do the next time you run across an error is to mark the page." She looked at me with a puzzled look. I then said, "Shut the book and read the title out loud - JUST GET OVER IT! You see, God did it on purpose to help you keep going and for you to see things don't have to be perfect to be good!" I couldn't believe I just said that to her. But you know, it is true and I needed to know that as well.

As I look back, I realize those errors almost made me stop sharing my book. All the effort and experiences I have had in my life might have stopped there. I wrote the book to help others on their own journey. But it certainly wouldn't help anyone sitting in my garage. With much encouragement from my friends, I knew I needed to go forward with this book.

To help me advertise the book friends did all kinds of cute things like making a carry bag and postcards with the book cover on it. One of my neighbors ended up being an editor. She re-edited the book to make it just like I wanted in the first place.

Yes, I will keep sharing the first edition to remind myself and others, **"Don't Give Up"** in what you believe. I made a choice to JUST GET OVER IT and trust God had a plan in the bad as well as the good He brought into my life - even my book.

I am once again reminded of Romans 8:28, *"And we know that God causes **ALL THINGS** to work together for good to those who love God, to those who are called according to His purpose."*

Publications with Susan's Inspirational Stories

"Women of Faith New Testament" 1997.

"Today's Christian Woman" with Connie Neal September/October 1998.

"Holding on to Heaven While Your Husband Goes Through Hell" by Connie Neal 1998.

"Chicken Soup for the Christian Woman's Soul" 2002.

"Comfort for the Grieving Heart" 2002.

"Chicken Soup for the Caregiver's Soul" 2004.

"Amazing Grace for Married Couples" 2005.

"Divine Stories of the Yahweh Sisterhood" 2006.

"Good News Northwest" November 2006.

"Praise Reports Volume Two" Inspiring Real-Life Stories of How God Answers Prayer 2006.

"Chicken Soup for the Nurse's Soul – Second Dose" 2007.

"Good News Northwest" February 2007.

"Good News Northwest" March 2007.

The Phoenix Society "Burn Support News" Fall 2007.

The Phoenix Society "Burn Support News" Winter 2007.

"Chicken Soup for the Soul – Happily Ever After" 2008.

"Chicken Soup for the Soul – Count Your Blessings" 2009.

Contact Susan Lugli

Susan Lugli shares her inspirational story all over the country to burn survivors, women's groups and church retreats. She still works with the Phoenix Society speaking at their annual World Burn Congress. She and her husband Rusty are active in their church and community.

To contact Sue about speaking to your group please contact: **http://www.susanlugli.com**. And visit Susan's blog at **http://susanlugli.blogspot.com/**.

Made in the USA
San Bernardino, CA
24 May 2017